POETRY STAINED LIPS

Other titles by April Y. Spellmeyer

Sacrifice & Bloom

Scars of a Warrior

ACCLAIMS FOR APRIL Y. SPELLMEYER

When I first started reading the poetry and prose of April Y. Spellmeyer, I was struck at how honest and gritty it was. So many unspoken things we go through and she attacked them outright and didn't try to make them pretty. Sometimes they aren't. And April has a beautiful way of speaking truth and letting you know she is there, and she sees you. She is so skilled at writing to her depression, abuse, sorrows and letting them know they aren't going to win. I'm so glad there is a writer who is brave enough to acknowledge the things we don't want to talk about. To sit with you in the dark times as well as push for growth and healing. Her words weave beautifully and hit with such raw emotion. She will teach you to be a warrior, and the story of her transformation will empower you.

Dawn P. Harrell — Author of Seasons of a Sewer Girl

April writes about honoring all versions of ourselves through darkness and light, and everything in-between; from the acknowledgment and acceptance of pain to the healing and growth that comes from it. April's words reminds us we aren't alone on this journey.

Kristin Kory

An exceptional poet - April will take you throughout life with its heartbreaking losses and greatest redemptions. Her words give hope to the hopeless and shine a light through the darkness so other may find their way out. She spills her ink in such a way, that even those who have not traveled the same path will know the fall and eventual rise of those that have. In the process of saving her own soul and speaking her truth she has helped others do the same. I know, for I am one of those she walked with until I found the light.

Kimberly Krausman

―――――――――――

April is an amazing soul and when you add her beautiful words to that, she's fire. She never ceases to amaze me with how unapologetically raw and honest she is and with every word she pens, I see a little bit of myself standing there. And with that I feel seen and heard a lot more than I did before. That's the magic of a writer and April absolutely nails it every single time. Her writing isn't the kind you'd just skim through, but every word pulls you in and somehow makes you feel much closer to yourself. We can all relate to April's journey and learn something along the way. I'm thankful to have April's words to accompany me on my journey, regardless of the season of my life I'm in.

Stephanie Bennett-Henry

Poetry Stained Lips from April Y. Spellmeyer is a collection of her three prior books of poetry and prose. April's writing is always authentic, accentuating a haunting sadness. Her writing reminds me of all of life's stages resonating with the flavors of nature throughout the seasons of the soul. Some of her words are Winter, chilling to the bone while others speak of Spring's hope and joy. April's stories are those of growth and perception and of feelings that must be borne.

One of my favorite pieces is "Rollercoaster…I didn't buy a ticket for this ride. It was forcibly thrust into my hand; a lifetime membership to ride this rollercoaster. There was a time when I knew to buckle up, but there have been plenty of times where I'm in full panic mode. Struggling to find the safety belt, to somewhat secure myself for what is about to come." She adeptly defines what it is like to be bi-polar while at the same time portraying how her warrior spirit continues to rise. Ups and downs, the description of life is all deeply and exquisitely expressed. It is why I am a big fan of April's writing and love seeing her own light smash through the shadows of depression as she continues her fight with writing that conveys absolute courage. I highly recommend Stained Lips, for her words are a refuge during those dark nights of the soul we all endure.

Kathy A. Tatay – Author of Kaleidoscope Heart

In Poetry Stained Lips, the newest book of poetry from author April Y. Spellmeyer, you will find a collection of short, medium, and long writings from this prolific author. April takes you on a ride with her words and you will experience every up, down, twist and turn of her thoughts and emotions through the use of her powerful, gut wrenching charged words. From writing about her struggles with bipolar to the triumphant joys of her victories – every piece is packed with raw emotion spilled onto the paper. Poetry Stained Lips is an amazing collection of raw truth from the author and is a great addition to her published works.

Hanlie Robbertse

POETRY STAINED LIPS

a collection of poetry and prose by

April Y. Spellmeyer

300 SOUTH MEDIA GROUP

NEW YORK | UNITED STATES

Copyright © 2021 by April Y. Spellmeyer
All rights reserved.

No part of this book may be reproduced in any form or by any electronic or mechanical means including information storage and retrieval systems, without permission in writing from the author. The only exception is for book reviews or articles written about the book and/or author.

This book is presented as a collection.

ISBN-13: 978-0-9970356-6-7

First Printing July 2021
Published by 300 South Media Group
Book Design & Layout | 300 South Media Group | 300SMG.COM

CONTENTS

Page 1   SECTION I - PASSION
Page 69   SECTION II - EMOTION
Page 139   SECTION III - INTENSITY

For Jeanne and Matty

my words are full-bodied lips draped in red velvet lipstick anticipating a lascivious kiss for my words to be devoured

April Y. Spellmeyer

Poetry Stained Lips

PASSION

give me my euphoric ride — i will not fight it this time i am ready to rise — take me higher than before — let me breathe in the chaos — at the beginning it always taste sweet — but then my thoughts scatter in the wind my voices are crystal clear and synced up — hallucinations both audible and visible at every turn — questioning my reality — i feel like i am going insane — energy levels at their peak — there is no need for sleep — it is just a waste of time — nothing can slow me down — i am invincible when i am on top — but all things come to an end — i will free fall — hurdling to the ground — wreckage of my psyche smashed — i cannot pick up my pieces yet — this is not over — part two is now beginning — this is always the hardest part — where my lungs will ache just to breathe i will feel lost — i need to find my bearings — i will not like being in my own fucked up skin — there is no escape — i will breakdown — i will shut down — i will be a cold hearted bitch — all because i forgot how to function — how to care for myself — my days and nights will blur — the tears will flow — the loathing sets in and drags me to rock bottom the pain becomes unbearable — sleep becomes my best friend — i just have to crawl a little further — just a little longer and then i will be okay — i always am — i always find a way — but there is always fear that one day maybe i will not be okay — all i can do is wait until the day comes for my next bipolar ride where i will have to decide once more — will i submit or will i fight

i am a magnet to melancholy and madness

will the day ever come for you when you are sifting through past memories — will your thoughts turn to me — remembering you broke my heart — leaving me scarred and broken — will you be filled with remorse or will you smile with pride i was another notch upon your belt

Poetry Stained Lips

i wanted to be
a ballerina
a firefighter
a movie star
a doctor
instead i let them change me
into trash
a whore
an addict
a lost cause
trauma carved into my bones
rage coursed through my veins
my heart pounded tragedies
i swallowed filth
filled my stomach with servings of disgust
i believed i would never be enough
until the day i mustered all my strength
never to allow them to have their hands
around my throat to silence my voice
i rose from the ashes and now they
tremble when i roar

with a shot of lachrymose and a chaser of heartache, i will drown all of love's memories

to escape from this out of tune world i get lost in music — every note, every lyric, every song takes me on a new journey no matter how many times i press play damn it all to hell — is there anyone who will ever lift this veil of strength to see i am in pain — no one wants to see the heaving of my chest or hear the catch in my throat — to take away all of my fears — fucking hell i wish my heart would stop at least for one beat to give me a moment of peace — just to be able to breathe one breath of relief instead of being in agony — i want to be caught as i fall — arms to be wrapped around me a kiss to the forehead and to hear the words just let it all out — i am here for but instead i sit here in the bathtub writing this as i taste the saltiness of my tears — i have to believe with time this will all pass but until then this is excruciating — i just have to keep holding onto the hope — that single strand which is barely shining in the darkness that surrounds me i wear a mask of i am fine - regurgitating nonsensical pleasantries as i bleed tragedies

she made hell into paradise – broken look flawless – madness became sane she wore her chains of tragedies as precious jewels – hiding behind her mask of pain

OUTSIDE LOOKING IN

I've never belonged. I have and often still feel as if I'm a pebble in the shoe of others. At first, not noticed, then a nuisance. Then finally removed to be casually tossed aside and forgotten. Needing to be purged from memory, a haunted soul that doesn't fit in.

Could it be possible this is what my fate has laid out for me? To be there to comfort, love, and give strength until they're ready to take their next step. I'm left abandoned on this lonely road of life's journey. I drift in this world, with no importance. Why does my presence become too much, causing my name to be spit out in disgust.

It hurts to know I'll always be on the outside looking in. I want to be a part of something, anything, just one time. Just give me five minutes to feel the warmth of belonging. Is that too much to ask?

Poetry Stained Lips

i feel ugly – i hate the skin i am in my soul feels bruised, my bones brittle from all the pain carved on them – i fight back tears – i tell myself do not do it – do not let them flow – it is a sign of weakness i bite my bottom lip hard until it is swollen – colors of blues and purples glistening with crimson – i take the back of my hand – smearing it across my lips, my cheek – as if i was trying to wipe away all traces of a bitter kiss i was forced to wear on my lips – the words i have swallowed are regurgitated until it fills my throat with the stickiness of filth and shame i taste it on my tongue but i am unable to purge the melancholy and madness i can only sit in silence as it devours me until i become an empty shell heartstrings are not meant for tug-of-war

i believed in fairy tales — once upon a time happily ever after at one time — i had it all until the villain of this tale cursed me — destroying the illusion of nothing could destroy us smashing it like a beautiful stained glass window being hit with a sledgehammer - pieces cutting me deep — leaving me broken and jaded — will i ever believe again even though it nearly killed me — damn right i will

Poetry Stained Lips

i did not want that day
the day you left me
my gift from fate was grief
|i lost my will to go on
fading into the shadows
becoming a shell of a person
draped in chains of misery
it hurt to breathe
i cried until my body ached
swollen eyes were my trademark
days and nights blurred
i sunk deeper into my depression
drowning in all the what-ifs
i was ready to welcome death
i was losing my mind
my only thought was to join you
nothing else mattered
i tried to make sense of it all
memories now haunt me
breathe
breathe again
those were the words
the sun rose to a new day
i knew i had to live
even if it was without you
little did i know

Poetry Stained Lips

this was the way to honor you
there is where i found my strength
in your love and memory
to begin again

do not just spill your ink - tattoo your words on the world

insomnia dusted with madness — downing whiskey drams and cigarettes — the taste of past regret fuel strands of the unknown, searching for a connection to keep the fire burning in my misunderstood soul the last time she prayed was when she was eight, when she was told there was no higher power who would ever save her

in between the blows she received, her welts became bruises, any belief she had was washed away with water and her blood she could only walk on eggshells while trying not to be seen or heard, knowing there were more atrocities to come

she had no choice but to try to pray one more time to pray to those who used and discarded her like a piece of garbage, hoping her prayers would be answered by them, in some sort of fucked up way

but those prayers went unanswered, it was not until she was torn to pieces, her body ruined, she realized she was the only one who could save herself if she wanted to live, to breathe without fear, her days of praying were gone - she had to become her own savior and wash away the sins of others from her flesh if she was ever to be whole again

TIRED WARRIOR

We have charged the battlefield with sword and shield all our years. Our strength feeling light as a feather most of the days. Then there are days they're too heavy to lift. Strength will abandon us from time to time. But all we can do is wave a white banner of surrender. We lay under the sun, gasping for breath with bruised bodies and bloodied lips, begging for it all to end.

Those days are the hardest, especially when you have been told over and over your strength never wavers. Sometimes it's a relief, to become weak and let go because being brave is exhausting. Have your doubts, your fuck it days, have your days of weakness, have your days of saying it's not fair. This doesn't make you less of a warrior. It just means you're a tired warrior needing to rest for now.

As we curse the gods with why me again. Your strength will slowly return. We refuse to be defeated and be told what to do. On bloodied hands and knees we'll cross endless miles until we can stand again. Our tears of hope will replenish our strength, becoming nourishment to fight another day. This may happen more than you can count, but always rise even if it's your last breath.

With time we hope our wounds will one day scar. We'll find the peace we've been fighting for. We'll be able to give our consul to new warriors just beginning to fight their battles. In the end, know you're a warrior. You've claimed your victories. You did it your way. You went out fighting, proving to yourself, the world you're a warrior leaving behind a timeless legacy.

we write what we know, what we have experienced there is a reason they call us tortured souls we write about things where it makes some people feel uncomfortable, our words at times puts a face to ugliness, how it exists in this world the way it has affected us - some have been quick to judge, assuming we are broken beyond repair calling us crazy, unstable, better beware - it is okay they call us those names, they just are not ready to see the truth behind our words, our stories, our souls; as ugliness continues to wage war, there are the ones rising up with us, as one voice to say ugliness exists - where we will never fight alone, standing side by side up in arms, for us that is true beauty and strength taking on each other's wounds as our very own — we bleed, cry and scream as one, we are warrior sisters and brethren - we are a warrior tribe, claiming victory on the battlefield - we have clawed, fought and claimed our voice - we will be damned to have it silenced - we have bled ink from our veins, ripped our hearts out onto parchment, cried enough tears to create new oceans - we will no longer cede to requests to water ourselves down to make you feel at ease - for it would be a disservice to us our words are our bandages to heal wounds - with the hope one day they will be healed - we no longer call ourselves victims nor survivors - we have transcended — we are warriors

colors i have painted in my world always fade leaving me to stand in shades of gray

the forbidden fruit in Eden was bitten bringing forth original sin but darlin' it does not even rival the wickedness on my flesh, my lips, my tongue, whispering sweet honey temptations in your ear as you plunge deep between my thighs begging for absolution of your sins i knew from the first time i shot up your love in my veins, i knew i was going to be hooked i never felt such pleasure or pain coursing through me — taking me higher every time but like any dealer, there was a price to pay — i willingly let you take pieces of my soul just to get another hit of blissful ecstasy, no resistance from me — i shoot up

when there was no more of me to give, where my flesh was rejected as payment, i hollowed out my soul, letting my life slip away — i became a junkie, i was fooled by what i thought was love, in the moments i was sober i realized they were lies in disguise

i crumpled to the ground with your needle of lies still in my arm, begging you to please stay, i will do anything, just give me one more hit, where i can pretend even if for a short time, your lies are really love

Poetry Stained Lips

there are moments when the only solace i can attain is baring my throat to the jaws of chaos

there were times in my life i treated certain events as a masquerade ball where i could don my i am fine mask knowing i would not be questioned — as time has gone by my i am fine mask is now a permanent fixture while the real me has been erased from all existence

Poetry Stained Lips

you say my words should be delicate and sweet, being able to savor them oh darlin' even if i could, i never would because i am not that way

i want you to taste the burn of my words when they pass your lips, making you swallow hard as your eyes water until they slowly rip you apart

you will then feel what rawness is what it is like every single time i split myself open, bleeding ink from my veins, revealing my wounds

REMINISCE

I used to be the person who tossed ticket stubs, flowers, cards, handwritten letters, and love notes in a memory box to mark that moment, to forever freeze it in time. It almost became a habit to toss little mementos into a box that was closed more than open.

We would say...we'll reminisce one day

Those mementos became less and less as time went on. The box was out of sight, out of mind, collecting dust. Maybe it was because we figured those mementos would be enough; where we wouldn't need them until we were much older, wiser, and when our memories became hazy.

We would say...we'll reminisce one day

We were busy planning a life together, we were going to do it all. Soon that box became a second thought. Why wouldn't it be a second thought, we had the world at our feet. We believed nothing could get in our way. We believed we had forever.

We would say...we'll reminisce one day

We had a spark that set the world on fire. We had people tell us they envied our love. Our love was a once upon a time kind of love; a love some spend a lifetime to find.

Even then it's still a one in an infinity chance. We had it, I don't know why fate chose us, but the fates did.

We would say...we'll reminisce one day

What we weren't told is that type of love is never meant to last. The rules of the universe made sure we ended in tragedy. Splitting us, scattering our love among the stars with hopes we never find each other again.

We could no longer say...we'll reminisce one day.

Those days will never come. The stories of how those memories made you feel will never be given breath to live. I have to hope I will be able to give them breath one day.

 Until then I say...I'll reminisce one day.

Poetry Stained Lips

i have tasted grief and it is bitter – it cannot be rinsed out of my mouth nor wiped off my lips no matter how many times i have tried – grief has changed me in a way to where a part of me died instantly but still kills me slowly over time i have felt grief's bitterness seep into my soul settling in my bones along with all the memories and what-ifs – then love came along one day after i fortified the walls of my heart – love breached them like a thief in the night – breathing new life and hope deep inside me – i threw caution to the wind and swore i would lay down my life a million times all in the name of love even when fear had its grip – i know i will lose again – death bides its time – waiting to collect the bounty of my love by ripping out my heart - stealing what remains – until then i will love until death gives me his kiss – that final kiss – extinguishing my flame

for every ounce of love coursing through your veins, there is a drop of pain waiting to break your heart

here i am opening old wounds that have long scarred all because i cannot resist the drug called nostalgia – breathing it all in – making me euphoric as it has me crawling on my hands and knees – begging for more of a love which was never meant to be

Poetry Stained Lips

that one night as the music played – i stood barefoot – wearing your shirt – swaying to the lyrics – you came up behind me – arms wrapped around my waist – pulling me close kissing my neck – you spun me around to where our eyes met – my head swirling from the intoxication of you – time stopped – the world for a moment was ours – kissing my lips – taking my hand to dance – you whispered in my ear i was yours and you were mine - soul entwined – and then our song and you fade away – reality sets in this was just a memory from the past

do not let their actions silence your truths

darlin' i know the loneliness that flows through your veins, your eyes filled with sadness highlighted red from your crying – the way you hold your hand to your heart trying to keep the pieces from falling away while nodding your head while taking a deep breath, choking back the tears to utter the words i am fine, when inside you are screaming for someone, anyone to see behind your mask i did not come from a line of brave women - they were all taught to be seen and not - heard — to carry traumas in bloodied hands with lips sewn to keep silent, passing them to the next set of innocent hands, staining them with the pains of the past without rhyme or reason — do i continue like my ancestors did — passing down unhealed wounds to daughters and sons of the present and future a burden they were not meant to carry — it was clear, i had to sever the ties of the past — birth a new ancestral line to heal lifetimes of wounds by rising from the ashes as a warrior with a spine of steel and a voice that no longer trembled but roared

PEDESTAL

Before you place me high on a pedestal, there are things you need to know. I'm not anything special, I have flaws, hell, I'm a collector of flaws. Only those closest to me have seen them up close and personal. Even then, some flaws have stayed hidden deep inside the caverns of my soul. They will never see the light of day as long as there is breath in me.

There was a time I caused heartache and pain all while walking away, leaving destruction in my wake. I refused to take the blame. I had a big ego back then, thinking I was better than some.

I believed I was this way because I was tired of being told all my life I wasn't shit and would never amount to anything. Believe me that small chip on my shoulder became like a boulder weighing down any chance to change.

Instead of love and receiving a tender touch, I choked on hate while rage fueled the fire inside my belly. It was the only way I knew. I allowed others to pull my strings even after they walked away.

My biting words were my defense to keep everyone at arm's length. I never wanted anyone too close and if they did; fuck I knew how to derail that train to happiness in a heartbeat.

Incredible writing this now, seeing how ridiculous I was. How I blamed others for what they did to me. I believed it was my free pass, my right to be an ugly person. Because of how I was treated, I thought fuck whoever got in my way, I would just run them over.

Maybe I changed because the years have passed, maybe because I was finally loved the right way, maybe because I was shown there was beauty in the world and more importantly in myself.

Beneath all the ugliness and muddied past, there was a flower struggling against the odds to bloom into something new and beautiful. It just needed care and time to get there.

I'm not proud of my past. I'm not proud of who I was. But I'm thankful for that one person who refused to give up on me, bringing me into the light. I was able to finally bury the ugly past and ugly parts of me. I was reborn, a new life, a new start.

Am I perfect? Fuck no. Will I ever be perfect? Fuck no. Who wants to be? I'm a better person today and will do my best the rest of my days.

But please, I beg you, never place me high on a pedestal. There is a part of me that will still jump. Darlin' don't make me risk it all to prove to you I still have flaws and can breathe.

I may be past the part in my life to be reckless, but I'll still prove you wrong.

Poetry Stained Lips

sitting here with the lights dimmed
tears fall from my red-rimmed eyes
i take a long drag off my cigarette
the ember glows as the paper burns
exhaling memories as the smoke swirls
my fingers caress a dram of whiskey
i swallow hard, tasting the burn
it is the only thing that keeps me warm
with furrowed brow, i try to remember
the lines in your face, taste of your kiss
sound of your voice, our bodies entwined
how my hand fit into yours, your breath
on my neck with whispers of sweet
nothings, the pain intensifies with every
heartbeat as the past and present collide
swallowing lost love and regret with
another dram, erasing what we once had

although she carried darkness she still illuminated the world

some days you have to put on the mask, fortifying your walls, rehearsing your most infamous line of i am fine with a forced smile, gritting your teeth while muttering fuck this world i am done – but you know you have to keep going even if you have to fake it just to make it another day – holding onto a glimmer of hope that it will be alright someday, one day; darlin' just keep going, you have a fire that rages within, keeping you alive – remember you got this

the day you took your last breath – my whole world
crumbled in an instant – a blur of loved ones –
heartbroken cries from our children – i numbed out –
death's fog enveloped me – the days after i laid on the
mattresses on the living room floor – where i slept before
when you were dying at home – i had a fear of sleep –
afraid i would never wake but yet i started to self-
medicate taking more and more to kill the pain – wishing
the next cocktail of pills and cocaine would let my life end
where i could be with you – i was slowly losing my mind –
barely going through the motions of what was yet to come
– the final goodbye – convincing myself at times you were
still alive – just another extended stay in the hospital –
waiting for you to come back home but it would never be
– you were gone – the day you were laid to rest was life
and death's cold slap of reality – this was not a horrible
nightmare seeing you in your coffin finally at peace – no
more pain – you looked like you were sleeping – i stayed
behind to have time with you – i cried and begged for this
not to be true – to please wake up – it was at that time
my heart and soul shattered – knowing my one true love –
my soulmate would be sending me home alone

i stitched my wounds with the cobwebbed memories of you

i have always believed to my core when i was told i was not good enough – even though those people are gone – they left their graffiti carved on my bones – now i doubt a kind word – a gesture from the ones who are genuine – i question if they have ulterior motives – fear begins to pound in my chest as it courses through my veins – fear beats like a drum in my head leaving me deaf to rationale – i become convinced they are only here to add to the mural of my graffitied bones

Poetry Stained Lips

remember every single moment we have – treasure them – keep them safe in your heart – remember every moment not just on the good days – but also the bad – because this is us perfectly imperfect our love remains constant – yet grows stronger every day – do not ever let go of a single moment of us because one day it is all that will remain – moments and memories sprinkled with pain because death had us part ways – we never know when it will come to a tragic end – this life will never be enough – we will never be able to stop the sands of time from falling – not one single grain – we often think like gods and we control our fate – but what we need to do is to keep seizing every moment and hold onto it with every single breath we take – when there are no more breaths to take – i want our moments left on my lips

LETTER OF A SUICIDE SURVIVOR

This will not be a pretty personal writing of what I have been through. I can now say I have had multiple attempts, but the past wouldn't allow me back then.

I won't sugarcoat my words of what it feels like to be helpless, hopeless. All those times I sat in silence without mentioning a word to a single soul I was not okay.

I didn't reach out when you're told to reach out. I just knew from my first attempt at twelve years old I would be judged as trying to get attention.

But you had it all wrong, I was hurting, I was in pain, I was lost, but most of all alone feeling I was a freak to want the pain to end. I would just be misunderstood and patted on the head everyone feels like this.

Fuck you not everyone feels like this, but there are too many to count that do. They walked the same path as I did. When you hear they died by suicide, from my own accounts and past; this was the one that took their life.

From my past attempts from age twelve to the age of forty-one I had one failed suicide attempt after another. From my personal experience, I guarantee by my opinion it was not their first attempt at suicide either. They did it in silence.

There are subtle things that could go on for days, months, or even years. You hide it well behind a mask you're happy, life is beautiful, and try to convince yourself just give it one more day. Maybe, just maybe, tomorrow will be alright. But we know it is a lie we try to convince ourselves of.

You see when we decide to end our lives. We want to reach out, but there is cruelty out there of here she goes again seeking for attention. So you plan and sit in silence; detailing every moment until the plan and time are perfect.

I don't know why after all my attempted suicides why I am still here. Maybe life's grand scheme won't let me cheat death before my time. So why does life decide to let others not survive? To be able to live, so maybe just one person will reach out, breaking the silence.

Those times I attempted, times I survived, I never spoke of it. All I could do is plan better for the next time. I wasn't going to reach out and once again be called an attention-seeking whore. Silence became my best friend.

Depression and mental illnesses have signs and symptoms. Did you know that depression's last symptom is suicide? It's called death by suicide when in reality it is death by the final stage of depression.

When I hear others say they were a coward to take their life. Don't you dare say that to me because you don't know their struggles, their pain, their anguish, the will to live slipping away. You didn't walk in their shoes, so you have no right to judge.

I know I felt shame for my attempts, the thoughts, the plans because everyone saw me as a mountain of strength. That nothing could break me. I knew I would be a disappointment, but at that point, you don't care except on how to end your pain.

My second to my last attempt was six years when my Christopher died. His death sent me over the edge of all my depression and grief that was built as a fortress. Did I reach out, no, instead I took a handful of pills only to be disappointed I woke the next day. Did I ask for help, no, silence once again was my best friend.

Please reach out no matter how hard it is, there is someone who is there to listen, to help, to get you to see a new day. It's ok to talk about it, to see a professional. I won't judge you; I will praise you for being here to take another breath.

My final plan was below for Wednesday, August 7, 2013, at 9:01 pm. This time I decided not to be silent and reach out. It taught me a valuable lesson. Reaching out does make a difference.

One person, one person reached out to me - to listen, to care, not to judge, it can make the difference between life and death. That one person changed my mind and gave me the reason to live after a lifetime of silence. This below was my cry for help.

Goodbye, Almost

This just hit me like a ton of bricks and took my breath away when I read it. As I'm going through journals/FB timeline for the grief book. I came across this:

Wednesday, August 7, 2013 @ 9:01pm
If any of my friends who suffer from bipolar 2 and/or depression, please PM. I'm having some real difficulty and need to talk to someone before tomorrow. No offense to anyone, I know you're all here for me and love you all. But I need someone who has "been there".

==========

That post right there was my goodbye to everyone. I had my plan the next day to end it all. I wanted to try one last time to see if anyone would reach out to me - to give me hope, give me a reason to keep living.

I had someone reach out to me and she didn't say a thing. She just listened to me - that night she saved my life. I didn't tell her until the end of the conversation that I was going to end it all the next day; but my mind was changed all because she listened. She will always be my hero.

That date, August 7, 2013, was the last time I have ever thought about ending it all. I still struggle, but I'm here - I'm breathing - I'm living and loving life.

once i was fooled on the honeyed words you spoke to me, believing every spoken word, every promise you made to me - as your words lingered on my lips and danced on my tongue, but when it was time to swallow them, the sweetness eroded leaving the taste of filthy deceit, having to choke them down ripping new wounds in my heart as my insecurities became resurrected but you never recognized this because my wounds were not visible, the illusions of love you projected lashed like a whip at my tender flesh, flaying it open not even then did you realize the pain you had inflicted

Poetry Stained Lips

there are times when my heart and mind need a translator to understand each other

never mind about the once upon a time and happily ever after — instead, let us travel down the rabbit hole to see how far it will go and create our own wonderland

i miss the days of handwritten love letters my heart would skip a beat – hands trembled in anticipation – butterflies fluttered within holding my breath – waiting to read words of love – desire – passion – begin seduced warmth of my body blushing – exhaling a sweet sigh of satisfaction – when it ends folding it gently – tucking it away – it only lasts a moment this time – unfolding it again as if i was undressing my lover caressing every fold – feeling it on my fingertips – becoming drunk on every single letter immortalized in the heart's ink on my soul i transformed my pain into butterflies setting it free to fly on wings of serenity

my kind are the poets, the songwriters, the musicians, the artists, the odd ones out, the 3 a.m. ramblers — where we become drunk on inspiration in each other's words, music and art not yet created — deep thought-provoking conversations fueled by whiskey, cigarettes and regrets while lighting our souls on fire

growth is like tending to a seed of a flower, if you are gentle you till the soil, give it a balance of sun, water and care it will flourish, blossoming into beautiful perfection, only if you have the patience if you rush its growth, it will not thrive, it will wilt, it will drown, it will die – the lesson here is do not hurry others to grow because you are ready for them to let them find their patch of soil, let them connect with the earth, water, and sky, let them plant their seed in their own time, let them heal their soul, let them find their peace because in the end you will be overjoyed you waited, you will be graced by their awakened beauty

POISON

All I have ever done was drink your poison. Your tongue cut me like a razor with your words; ripping apart my psyche as you saw fit.

Flesh and blood didn't mean a thing to you. I might as well have been an orphan. I competed with every breath to gain some acceptance, some sense of pride, for you to see something in me. But you always made sure to let me know I want and never would be good enough.

Dragging me through the mud with your lies, all I ever wanted was your love. I have concluded you can't and never will be able to love, but especially to love me.

Little do you know or even care, I have broken the cycle before of the atrocities you made me endure. Now I break the cycle of you.

I rise from the ashes as a mighty warrior. There is no hope or forgiveness to bestow upon you. You will be erased, forgotten, a hazy memory.

I no longer drink the poison you serve.

nothing good happens after 2 am - drinking too much until i was spinning, bringing home another one-night stand to be able to feel something, anything; the honeyed lies spilled from my lips, convincing myself i would be whole by another meaningless fuck until the morning when i would wake to an empty bed because i never let them stay that hole in my chest was bigger than the night before, looking in the mirror seeing bloodshot eyes, smudged eyeliner and remnants of lipstick smeared, while trying to figure out how i ended back at rock bottom once again; oh yeah now i remember as i put myself together just to do it all over

Poetry Stained Lips

i wish the memories of you could be erased like chalk on the chalkboard

i have watched her forge her crown — seize her throne — rearrange the stars to make her own destiny — a queen who never averts her eyes when she stumbles — instead, she rises up straightens her crown — head held high with unwavering courage and grace — do you know who this is — it is you — beautiful soul you are that queen — you always have been and always will be when you first look at me you would not believe all the battles i have endured behind this mask is where i keep hidden past failures and triumphs – my body, mind and soul has remnants of battlefield wounds which bled profusely – now you would have to pull back my many layers of battle-worn armor to see how those wounds have now scarred – remember looks can be deceiving because most of us are fighting a war without being seen or speaking a single word

there were times i was both arsonist and firefighter when it came to love

they were cruel as they watched her words become lodged in her throat watching her gasp for breath — they mocked her by making choking noises, laughing as her eyes filled with tears of panic — they towered over her as she fell to the ground — they exchange wagers on which breath will be her last breath for her to be silenced once and for all

Poetry Stained Lips

i want to know all the stories behind your scars the pain – the struggle – the way they were inflicted – how your beautiful soul was torn apart – tell me how you battled through it all even the time you were defeated – the times you wanted to give up – tell me how you rose up on your battlefield of pain and became victorious – those are the stories i want to hear so i can understand why you are here standing on my battlefield by my side – leading the charge for me to claim my victory

TIME

Our lives are ruled around time, those tiny grains of sand slipping away. I have still yet to let those grains of sand slip away. I know better, but I refuse to bend the knee.

Maybe I should still let those grains of sand escape because of the gods who no longer exist. But a thread of them woven into my soul, showing fate, time, and death I'm greater than gods.

How arrogant of me to have a god-like ego to challenge fate, life, and death. Yet again, instead of seizing the moment to wage a war of revenge of what was taken too soon.

Fate, time, and death will have me submit one day. It's a war I can't win, but I'll be damned to not go without a fight, inflicting pain.

Is it because I'm a warrior of tragedy? Is my grief turning more bitter with every breath? Is it because my soul is wild and free, not abiding by a cosmic plan?

I will not quit; I'll challenge those gods. I'm going to make the rules. I'll do things my way. I'll tell fate and death to fuck off as I seize time by the throat to bend it to my will.

for years she carried ugliness deep within her bones – scars upon her flesh – bleeding wounds she stitched closed with strands of hope to keep her soul intact – when she looked in the mirror with swollen eyes from all the crimson tears she has cried – a reflection of a stranger stared back at her – she was an empty vessel – she knew there had to more than to just exist – she had to let herself die to break the chains of pain she wore elegantly and tragically – with a deep breath she inhaled the flames – burning away the years of misery and pain – ashes fell like rain around her feet freeing her at last – this time she held the key to her fate as she rose as a mighty phoenix

Poetry Stained Lips

beneath breast and bone is a warrior's heart beating fire

you have seen me change – i have made amends – i have begged for forgiveness and at times i was denied – where i had to forgive myself as i swallowed the truth of my ugliness – but i have transformed into someone better – now i leave you with these questions – will you ever forgive me of my past or will you remain there to throw it in my face and miss out on the person i have become i often visit the graveyard of broken hearts to bury another piece – walking among the rows of headstones show me the past – reminding me of the pain i once felt – there was a time when i would be on my knees begging the gods to let it all end only to be denied – the times where i thought it would kill me – the agony of feeling each heartbeat being silenced as i carved it out of my wounded heart – burying them alone – deep into the ground – laying them to rest in hopes peace will be found – now when i visit i place pretty flowers upon the headstones – trying to find some beauty in the broken pieces which no longer live or bleed

one cannot blossom among barren hearts and dehydrated souls

there have been many nights when the world slumbers and my demons are roused — they sift through my heart — inflicting new wounds and flaying open old scars — i feel the pain well up and feel the catch in my throat — no longer able to fight back the floodgate of tears my chest heaves as i fight for my next breath treading through the waves of heartache as my demons pull me under — trying to drown me in a tsunami of regrets and what-ifs when we first met and started our love affair we captured our love through photographs the love you could see in our eyes – we had forever – as time went on our photographs became less – then the day came and you took your last breath – now you were gone and i searched for photographs of us – i wanted to remember happier times – to forget the grief because my memories could not be recalled as easily – when those photographs were found there were too few how could we only have a handful of photographed memories – time was stolen from us – the years without you have taken a toll on me – our photographs rips wounds open – with no choice i have to put them all away with the hope one day i will be able to smile instead of cry about the lovers we once were

DARKNESS

Do you think I ever get tired of ripping my chest open to pull out the darkness? To constantly open my wounds, bleeding tragedies once again. All because I try to find some headway to walk in the light of beauty. Instead, I'm bound by the chains of darkness.

I know there is light somewhere deep inside my soul. I would love to feel light's warmth on my fragile shell. I fear what lies between the light and me. I know I have to travel through the darkness to reach for the light.

I loathe the darkness like I did as a child who was locked in a room without a ray of light, no hope. I could only beg, please let me out. Now my light is begging, screaming to be set free. Only for darkness to envelope my lost light with its icy claws.

I try to strap on my armor, but it's too heavy to wear. It confines me, making it hard to breathe. I just can't go into battle once more. I'm tired, I'm worn, I'm bloodied from my past wars.

Today I'll submit. I'll allow my demons to pick me apart, strip me to where there is only bone and marrow. I know it is a painful price to pay, but today I'm willing to pay it.

i want you to kiss me the way the moon kisses the ocean

i used to long to be someone's muse – i believed it would be romantic – poems written filled with eternal love and desires then i fell in love with the written word no longer wanting to be a muse – to be stripped naked in front of the world walking the razor's edge where you could be loved – lusted – hated – die and resurrected – sometimes all wrapped into one – time and time again – hoping you will not be damned – having your soul stained by the ink bled out from their veins onto parchment – the love – the pain of memories still in their tender heart while being immortalized

Poetry Stained Lips

she was not the one to play damsel in distress waiting for a king to come charging in on his white steed – sword drawn – ready for battle he just assumed she needed to be saved – she was a prize to be won with the notion she wished for a once upon a time as compliant queen instead she was the sort who charged into battle body covered in war paint – creaming her warrior song with fierceness in her eyes – strength in the way she wielded her sword – slaying her enemies as she crowned herself queen – seizing the throne forging her own fairy tale ending of happily ever after as a warrior queen

every now and then pain has been my intimate consort

do not promise me tomorrow because tomorrow may never come – do not tell me forever because nothing lasts forever just give me today – love me – hold me give me tender kisses that is all i need and if tomorrow is to come please do it all over again

Poetry Stained Lips

i have traveled along this lonely treacherous road far too long — melancholy and madness have been my constant travel companions — never leaving my side when everyone else has faded away — i believe they will guide me — to show me the way — to find my way back home — but i know the risks with melancholy and madness — i know they will not make it an easy road for me — they will inflict wounds just to watch me hemorrhage pain — but they have also sewn back the tender parts of me when i do not what to do with all the pieces coming undone at the seams — will i continue this road with them will a day come when there is a fork in the road will i choose to take the high road to find my inner peace — or will i take the low road until i am crawling on bloodied hands and knees — begging the gods to take me — at times i do not know except i have to take the next step — to keep my foot upon path even it is on this lonely treacherous road — i will keep hope grasped in my hand — that one day — someday i will say goodbye to melancholy and madness while saying hello to peace — i just hope it is not with my final breath as it escapes from my quivering lips

melancholy gives my madness the solace it desires

what does grief taste like
it tastes like salty tears
bittersweet memories

what does grief feel like
it feels like dying
your heart ripped out whole

how do you live with grief
with every ounce of strength
you can muster – sometimes
a moment at a time

how do you survive grief
with every painful breath
until your light is extinguished

open the door to my soul and i will show you galaxies waiting to be discovered

i hide behind a mask – choking back grief until i can cry in the dark where no one can

see my tears – i torture myself with all the what-ifs – playing back memories of us like

an old movie picture – my wounds bleed – i am unable to stop the crimson flow through my bandages – staining my soul i am haunted by the ghost of you – i wonder if this is real or if i am in hell – i walk the thin line between past and present – never knowing where i truly belong

UNSPOKEN TRUTH

Hello depression we meet again. I know how this all goes down between you and me. I've been waiting for you. Come slide between the covers with me. Wrap your arms around me, let me breathe in the sadness while I choke down the tears filling my throat. My mind is foggy, and I can't think rationally when you are next to me. You constantly whisper how much of a burden I am, reminding me of every mistake ever made. I don't even try to resist you because I know it's all true.

All I can do to quiet you is to sleep, to sleep away the hours where I don't want or have to feel anything. I wake and you're still next to me. I toss and turn to get back to sleep. The sun peeking through the curtains as if it's wanting to help me escape the darkness I'm wrapped in. I pull and arrange the curtains to keep the light out, my eyes can't handle the brightness, the warmth.

I chew my nails down even further where the skin is torn, fingers raw. I debate what i should do next; frustrated I finally find the will to get out of bed. But you are my shadow, following me. My chest heaves with every breath, with every heartbeat, my body sore. Maybe if I try to brush my hair, it will be a start. But every stroke is painful. I look in the mirror trying to convince myself I'm staring at a stranger. Your cold hands on my shoulders, forcing me to

Poetry Stained Lips

see it's me. My face is swollen from crying about things I can't put into words. My lips dried out, cracked from lack of hydration. My skin all red and splotchy, nose running. Forget about taking a shower because the water feels like it's ripping me open. I'll just put on some deodorant. It will have to be enough.

I shuffle through the house becoming lost. Maybe I should eat. Now the thought of food is nauseating. The thought of one morsel of food touching my tongue makes me gag.

What was I going to do, fuck I've already forgotten. Honestly, I really do not fucking care as I slam cabinet doors shut. I catch a glimpse of my t-shirt and the stains. I figure it has been days since I have changed my clothes.

Maybe some music; the playlist titled sadness. Skipping song after song until the right one drives like a dagger to my stomach. Playing it on repeat, listening to it 10, 20, 30 times. Oh that part right there, those lyrics had to be written for times like this.

Here I go again with the tears and the oh why this and that. I sink into you with hopes you will give comfort, but you just lead me to more darkness. Fuck I hate it when you overstay, especially since it was forced, or at least that is what I tell myself. But there are always signs.

Maybe I should call someone, text someone, message someone; you whisper are you fucking serious? No one cares especially for you. You will just give the line you're fine and force happiness in your voice while sewing your lips closed. Where the truth will not spill out that I'm truly a fucking mess. As always I respond with, you're absolutely right. I'm going back to bed and you follow me.

Another day, another night, another day, another week, sometimes longer. The cycle seems endless. A ride with no stops. Your arms around me, squeezing the will, the hope, out of me. All I can do is go to sleep, whispering I surrender. Please go and be done with me. The day does come, you finally leave by your choosing, taking your darkness, saying goodbye. But always reminding me you'll be seeing me sooner than later.

Poetry Stained Lips

what can i write that i have not written before how many more ways can i say my grief swallows me whole — how my heart aches from the very thought of you — the what-ifs and regrets still bitter in my mouth even after all these years no matter how much ink bleeds from my veins it all comes out the same — are my past transgressions the consequence of losing you before i made amends for all i did wrong for all the things left unsaid — for all the i love you's that got caught in my throat as my tears took over — for the broken promise i would be there to hold your hand as you were to face the unknown is this how it is to be — is this who i am — will my remaining days be bound in chains of regret to this mortal world — will it be enough of a sentence served for when my last breath is taken i will be freed and you will be there waiting for me

EMOTION

she made angels sigh and demons blush the way she wore purity and sin

hurtful words are ammunition being loaded on the tips of tongues as turbulent emotions rise — it does not matter who shot first — the casualties are two hearts caught in the crossfire tourniquets for wounds inflicted become a bloodstained white flag of surrender as both sides lose each other as the tears begin to well up in the corner of my eyes - the lump forms in my throat to choke back the pain of heartache trying to force its way through already bruised lips from the last time i lost the fight with my demons - they came disguised as love, hope and life to release razor sharp shards of grief - bringing them to life - cutting my lips deep unable to scar - leaving me to taste the constant reminder of sticky saltiness of blood and agony with every single breath - my fingers become as claws ripping open my chest to rip out what is left of this dying heart - holding it in my dirtied hands of the blackened sins of what-ifs - knowing i will never receive absolution even though my blood courses contrition through my open veins - unable to cease the flow of words spilled onto paper - i walk on scorched feet through the fire of my personal hell - the smell of brimstone penetrates and intoxicates as i crumble to my knees with arms outstretched unable to scream from the fire i breathe - begging, needing, wanting my last breath to be silenced from death's cold calculating kiss - my mortal shell now an empty vessel - my bones ground into ash - my soul is freed for an instant until it is chained to purgatory all because i held onto the hauntings of my memories instead of burying them in peace as they were meant to be

a dandelion field of endless wishes

love letters written in the sand under the stars that cling to the black velvet sky, the ebb and flow of gentle waves slowly erase my words of love — carrying my message upon their crest — the wind blows through my tresses, smell of the salt air puts me in a trance — closing my eyes i make a wish this night will be the night your soul will be out there to catch my love before the moon kisses the ocean farewell

never let anyone tell you to let go of your pain - it is not up to them - your healing is not bound by the tick of a clock - it is not checked off like an item on a to-do list - it is not a scheduled appointment
healing is messy, ugly, consuming
heal your wounds
free your pain
find your peace
on your time
on your terms

ROLLERCOASTER

I didn't buy a ticket for this ride. It was forcibly thrust into my hand; a lifetime membership to ride this rollercoaster. There was a time I knew when to buckle up, but there have been plenty of times where I'm in full panic mode. Struggling to find the safety belt, to somewhat secure myself for what is about to come.

No need for sleep because of the intoxication of riding this high is too much of a temptation to deny. I'm drawn to it like a moth to a flame. I know I'll get burned, but I still ride. The hours turn to days and then to weeks. Never wanting it to end because of all I can achieve even while fighting my demons. I'm invincible when I'm at the top, looking down, chest puffed out, strategizing my next move of what I can conquer next.

I'm always surprised when I begin to spiral out of control; getting ready to crash into a fiery piece of wreckage. I try to crawl, but this part of it makes it painful just to breathe. Now the darkness creeps in, reminding me I'm not good enough, whispers resonate in my head I'm not right. I'm fucked up, damaged goods. But it's the price that comes with this and I pay it in full every fucking time.

All I can do is lie here and stare at these four walls. Sadness consumes my soul, leaving me cold and alone. It feels like an eternity until it's time to ride it once more.

I'm a glutton for punishment and out of control. I hesitantly climb back on knowing it'll kill another tender part of me.

Poetry Stained Lips

i have playlists just for writing – those songs may not mean anything to anyone else but they mean everything to me – each song transports me back to the moment in time where i felt every single word belted out – earbuds in – volume up to drown out the world – replaying the same song for hours on end – healing me – mending my broken heart – overwhelming emotions in those three to four minutes still leaves me breathless even after all these years – pressing play once again – listening to those songs to see if i missed another meaning or has it changed my love for those haunting lyrics imbedded in my soul – words escape me as to how i feel is eloquently written from someone else's pain which gives me solace i am not alone – the way they can make their words flow in perfect rhythm – at times it feels those words were written for me – as the lyrics wash over me – opening me up – becoming inspired – i begin to sing those songs with pen in hand – the words begin to flow like blood from my veins mixed with salty tears staining the parchment – forever immortalized i create my own song

if i am ever to have inner peace — i must let go of the sins
i have carried for others

the words which hurt the worst were the ones that got
caught in my throat, choking me — unable to give them life
from my breath — if only they would have fallen from my
lips, maybe our love would have been saved instead of
shedding tears of grief while burying our broken hearts in
a graveyard of regrets

Poetry Stained Lips

have i failed — hell yes i have — i have perfected the craft — i have been defeated — thrown to my demons for them to feast upon the tender parts of me more time could ever count — i have been thrusted into one tragedy after another — i have cried, begged, cursed the gods as i have been knocked down and left wounded but i keep going even if it is on bloodied hands and knees i will crawl for miles until i can stand again becoming stronger than before — i will not give up because it has and will never be an option

when loneliness pours like rain it washes away all the colors in my soul

tragedy is her dealer, she craves for another syringe filled with nostalgia, giving a piece of her shattered heart for payment – she swears this is the last time; she knows it will be a short-lived high, it is a risk she is willing to take without hesitation she injects it into her vein the longings of her past has become her future

Poetry Stained Lips

it has been quite a while since we had time to sit sipping coffee casually – removing our masks for the afternoon – letting our demons come out and play together like children running free on a playground – our conversations are so matter of fact – like we were discussing the latest trend when it is all about the time we clawed our way out of hell – we have those a-ha moments and do you remember the time this or that happened recounting the wounds that are brand new and wounds which have scarred – by the end of the day we put our masks back on – call out to our demons to come inside – while parting ways to go back to our own personal hell – i turn to wave goodbye only to realize you were never here – all of this was just the voices in my head – skewing my reality once again

WEARING PAIN

Some of us wear pain as wounds on the flesh, some try to drown it all in a bottle, some go numb, some put up walls, some hide it behind a smile, some suffer in silence, some just become invisible, some cry alone.

There is one thing which is the same for everyone. We want love, understanding, and waiting for an outstretched hand. We want to be reminded we aren't alone.

I was always told my pain wasn't and isn't that bad. To just let it go because I did survive. It's not that easy to just let it go. Long after the wounds were inflicted, the pain still remains as bleeding, gaping wounds.

My pain is no less than anyone else's. My pain could be too much for someone and vice versa. We all feel different and our levels of strength vary across a vast spectrum of experience and how or when we decide to heal from our pain.

The common thread we all have with pain is we want to heal our wounds. Some wounds will be healed and left as a scar. The scar a reminder of what we overcame. But there will be some wounds that will never heal and have to be cared for until your last breath.

I know I used to be ashamed of my pain. I used to keep it tucked away, deep in the caverns of my heart and mind. I

Poetry Stained Lips

was a master at wearing the mask and saying my rehearsed line of I'm fine.

But now I wear my pain as priceless gems around my neck. Hope sprinkled like stardust on my skin for all the world to see. My pain will never be locked away again. I will not be ashamed. I will speak my truth – my pain, just like yours deserves to be known.

i believed i could change you if i loved you enough – i stayed prisoner to your rage the ugliness you released upon me time and time again where i was compliant to learn a lesson you said i needed to be taught – i was the one who caused you to inflict wounds and i still crawled back on hands and knees begging you to please stay – i would thank you for setting me straight – apologizing over and over for making you angry – i had to prove to you by wearing the pain – the bruises – the scars – then it would show you how i would always be yours – what a mind fuck you put on my psyche – making me believe i could not live without you – even though i knew you were killing me with your fists – your words – then the day came and i said no more and found the courage to walk away even though i was broken but i was free never mind about finding your soulmate get out there and find your weirdo

i swallowed filth and called it nourishment i begged on bloodied knees and called it devotion i bent the knee and call it loyalty, i ripped open my chest and called it love, i cried oceans of tears and called it cleansing, i bled ink of unspoken words and called it contrition, all those things i did for you without hesitation, it was not until you broke me when i realized you and i were not meant to be but a hard lesson to be learned

Poetry Stained Lips

i swallowed your words — tasting the filth on my tongue — unable to breathe as i choked them down — red-rimmed eyes shadowed with hues of black, blues, and purples — lips crimson and swollen — you used your fists like a paintbrush — spilling my blood onto a canvas — as if you were trying to paint a masterpiece — i was on display to hear all the whispers of how can she stay — she has to be the one to blame — you took pride and wanted accolades — shame consumed me i was the only one to hear the screams in my head — i learned to walk on eggshells perfection became my name so i would not upset you — i stayed even though i knew it was wrong — believing if i could scrub away your fingerprints from my flesh maybe you would then change your ways — instead, you waited until your canvas was healed to paint upon it once again

Poetry Stained Lips

I drank from your lips until i became love drunk and i knew then i never wanted to be sober again

i have spent a lifetime letting others dress me in costumes and masks; inventing me into characters they deemed necessary – i would fit into their box of who they wanted me to be – i allowed them to write my script, rehearsing the lines they wrote, becoming an eloquent reciter as i stood on their stage waiting for their cue to project a false image of myself, convincing the world of something i was not all because I wanted acceptance darlin' i know you are hurting – you feel lost – your soul pierced – heart weary – the weight of the world on your shoulders leaving you to brace yourself believing if you take one more breath – one more step you will be crushed – i feel you are about to break – break without fear – there are times you have to break before you can go on – it is almost like a trust fall – so darlin' trust – just fucking break i swear until my last breath – i will catch all your pieces – i will catch you when you fall – i will be your voice when words fail you – i will see you rise from the ashes with a new sense of hope – i will feel your light course through your veins – healing your soul – bringing peace to your heart until the light bursts from your chest – making you whole while giving you enough grit to finish the fight and when you ask how can you believe this – all i can say darlin' is i learned long ago the most tragic breakdowns do become the most beautiful breakthroughs – the only difference between you and i is you do not have to do it alone

HARD LESSONS

If I would have known these things longs ago, long before I lost to death, lost to grief. I would've appreciated and treasured things more; even though I thought I did. But instead, I was taught hard lessons.

I should've seized time instead of wasting it. Watching it tick away. Instead of rolling my eyes, waving my hand that I will have more time when it was convenient for me. Because I believed in my youth time wouldn't affect me. Those times I can never get back no matter how hard I try to stop time now.

I swore never again would I allow my heart be put out on a limb. To be plucked for someone to love. I should've embraced every single moment even when it hurt, broke, and bruised my tender heart. My image of love shattered. It was to be a fairy tale. Fairy tales and once upon a time never leads to a happily ever after. The happily ever after is in the once upon a time and only for the living.

I would have forgiven more; I would have told my ego to take a hike. I would've forgiven even if it was just for more to heal and move on.

I should have loved harder, expressed it more. I would've said I love you a million and one times more because in the end it was still not said enough.

When death and grief grips, these are the things they take: their smile, their love, their kisses, their hugs, their heartbeat, their voices, stolen moments, holding hands, being together, growing old

Instead, we are left with the what-ifs, faded memories, pictures, broken heart, endless tears, grief, loneliness, guilt, emptiness, but the worst of all is the waiting.

Poetry Stained Lips

i have playlists of songs – some are for me to write to some are for reminiscing – some are for when i am lonely – some are for the loves i had – some are for heart break – some are from when i failed – some are for wishes unanswered – some are just to dance to some are for to smile – some are for passion – some are for me to shed tears – some are for my mental illnesses – some are for the what-ifs, could haves and should haves – some are for piercing my soul – some are for my breakdowns – some are for my breakthroughs some are for opening old wounds – some are for healing me – some are for the here and now – some are for chasing dreams – some are for things left unsaid – some are for when i was wrong – some for the goodbyes never said – some are for the nights i cannot sleep and i overthink – some are for me to breathe – some are for a new chapter – some are for long journeys walked alone – some are for sharing some are just for me – some are for making new memories – some are anthems to keep me going some are for times of weakness – some are for when i have strength – some are for when i do not have the words that i cannot grasp – some are for those gone too soon – some are for late night promises made and then broken when the sun rises – some are for just because – but every single note, lyric, and song they tell my story if you take the time to listen to them – only then you will know and understand who i am even when my soul is silent, you can hear its unspoken words between the beats of my heart

i have a graveyard of where love has died i visit there from time to time – bringing flowers to see if their beauty will erase the melancholy i still have – with each flower i place them on the graves – a moment of silence – my ghosts still roam – forever bound in the past and present – wailing their song of words left unsaid – i wonder when my day comes and my last breath is taken – will my ghosts be able to rest in peace or will i take my place among them have you ever wanted to let the floodgate of tears flow – instead, you fought them back by swallowing the hard lump in your throat – feeling like you were going to choke on bittersweet pain – looking up to the sky with hope the sun will dry up the tears filling your eyes – biting your lip so hard you tasted blood – forcing a smile while uttering the infamous line of i a fine – all because they have convinced you that you are the strong one and we all know the strong ones never break, right – you hold back like you have a thousand times before instead of asking for a moment of their time – you will wait until 2 a.m. when the world is asleep – you will step into the shower and sit in the corner embracing yourself with hope it will provide some sort of comfort – but all it does is remind you of how alone you are when your strength has abandoned you – water rushes over you letting you know now is the time – let it out – let it go the water will muffle your cries while washing away the tears – leaving only a taste of salt to remind you of your pain – you watch as your tears, pain and water all mix together as it circles the drain and disappears – you wish they could see you at this moment to finally know – to understand even the strongest struggle to survive like the stellar collision of two stars — our souls were destined to become as one

it becomes more difficult every day to find beauty in this world — ugliness has taken root — it has strangled beauty slowly and painfully — where you have to search harder for even a glimpse of beauty — knowing one day it will become extinct — no wonder hearts become hardened over time — filling the days with misery and grief — knowing in the end that ugliness will end up being the only beauty to exist

Poetry Stained Lips

standing in a field – feeling the gentle breeze - eyes closed in absolute silence – you come up and wrap your arms around my waist – you chin resting on my shoulder as you whisper what are you doing – i smile open my eyes and point to the sky – i say look at all the stars – the beauty of them that you cannot see from the city – you asked if i am going to make a wish and i laugh telling you i can only do that if there are falling stars – in that moment two stars brighten the sky – side by side – you say hurry make your wish i close my eyes and make my wish – you ask what i wished for and i tell you it is for us to be like this forever – i turn to you – embracing you – my head on your chest – i ask you what was yours – you kiss my forehead and say it was to have this moment with me – before i could say a word i begin to feel your embrace disappear – i cry – begging you to please stay - you tell me this was all fate could give us – this place between dreaming and where soul reside when they leave this mortal world – i wake aching for you – hearing your voice fading – tears flowing – i am once again left alone with our memories and the hope i will see you soon again in my dreams

ROSES AND THORNS

Damn who left the cage unlocked to release my demons for them to wreak havoc? Oh, that's right, it was me. Was I being careless or was it out of curiosity to see if I could outrun them this time? I try to elude them by running into an endless maze of roses and thorns I have created in my mind. What a beautiful place I have designed to keep out the ugliness.

At first, I am relieved knowing somewhere there is sanctuary; at least that is what I want to believe. But then my heartbeat begins to quicken. I gasp for breath as the panic begins to fill my throat; suffocating me slowly. My silent screams are unheard as crimson tears begin to flow.

I go deeper into this endless maze. I become disoriented, my mind racing with thoughts; was it a left I took, no, maybe it was a right. Fuck! I created this place; I should be able to remember the layout like the back of my hand.

I try to find the beacon of light to show me the way, to feel its warmth. But darkness closes in and looms like storm clouds and I grow cold.

I look around to see I am lost. I begin to claw at the maze walls; ripping handfuls of petals while crushing and bruising them. The thorns tear at my tender flesh. The

Poetry Stained Lips

smell of blood and the fragrance of roses become mixed leading my demons to me.

I become ensnared in the wall of thorns, unable to escape. Then reality begins to settle in, there was never any freedom from my demons. They know me all too well. They know my defenses, my weaknesses. It was just another game of hide and seek I was meant to lose. Freedom is just a bittersweet taste upon my bruised lips and reminds me these chains my demons hold will never break.

i apologize
i have apologized my whole life
i apologized when i was right
i apologized for my feelings
i apologized when i was hurt
i apologized for my beliefs
i apologized when i started over
i apologized when i found my voice
i apologized for my mental illnesses
i apologized in finding my inner peace
i apologized for shitty "friends"
i apologized for my independence
i apologized when i cried
i apologized for my strength
i apologized to keep the peace
i apologized for apologizing

i will no longer apologize for these

apologies rescinded

in a world full of uncertainty — do not let compassion go extinct

karma opened its book, coming to my name giving me back pain ten-fold for my past mistakes — even though i have begged for forgiveness and bled with every single breath day after day, month after month, year after year — to make all my wrongs right, karma is not satisfied — it sits me at its table, serving me plate after plate choking on every bite, i know this is the only way — i will sit there until karma says enough and excuses me from its table

when she is gone will he ever think of her - will he shed tears of pain and loss when those songs play on the radio they used to sing to — will he scroll through old text messages, reading and re-reading all the times she was being silly — will he go through old cards she sent him where she wrote how much she loves him while pledging her devotion and loyalty — will his heart be broken because when he dials her number and she is not there to answer

will he still watch the same shows or movies they used to cuddle up to — will he miss her being wrapped up in his arms — her head on his chest as she would drift off to sleep to the sound of his heartbeat — will he wish he could have just one more day with her — to tell her all the things he never told her — what will he miss about her — will it be her wild spirit, her loving nature, her warrior strength, her laugh, her sarcastic wit, the way her eyes lit up when he spoke her name, the way she smiled when he said i love you

maybe the real reason is he will miss just being around her — she was the only one that made him feel loved and alive — more than anyone ever did or ever could

Poetry Stained Lips

warriors are born on life's battlefields

nobody knows who the forgotten girl is, she is the one who is a hazy memory, nobody keeps her around for too long, she is a wisp of smoke from a blown out candle, but she still takes the risk and wears her heart upon her sleeve even though she knows it will be flayed open time and again, she weeps as she sews her wounds, tracing the crooked stitches and the scars from the past with bruised fingertips, her words linger on the tip of her tongue, her words denied breath and she swallows the decay, filling her throat with filthy bitterness — as much as she denies it, she knows who she is because nobody ever hears, nobody ever sees, nobody ever loves, nobody ever remembers the forgotten girl

she turned
her tears into diamonds
her demons into charms
her thorns into a crown
her screams into a song

she wore
her blood as lipstick
her scars as jewelry
her bruises as art
her broken heart
on her sleeve

she made her tragedies look
beautiful by the way she
carried them effortlessly

and this is why no one
will ever be able to see
her pain and suffering

SEVEN YEARS

I reflect back on these past seven years. These last seven years without you. You were my entire world. You were the first one who was ever gentle with me. You showed me what love was. You showed me the world could be a beautiful place, even in the smallest of things. You wanted nothing from me.

When you died, you left me, I became filled with hate. I didn't hate you, I hated myself. I hated myself because I couldn't keep you here. To keep you safe, the way you kept me safe. I never revealed to the world the hate was feeding on me, chewing me to bits.

I couldn't breathe, I couldn't sleep, I couldn't eat. I became self-destructive with pain pills with chasers of white lines. I perfected the art of spiraling down into darkness. I didn't care if I would live or die. Dying is what I wanted.

No one saw the real pain, the grief, they only saw what I wanted them to see. I knew how to wear the mask of I'm fine so fucking well. All those years before you died, I rehearsed that line, perfected the art of wearing masks.

I wanted to wail like a fucking banshee. Attack like a wild animal. Destroy what was around me. But all I could do is silently scream with fist clenched, nails cutting into my flesh, bleeding while my teeth clenched to where it felt my jaw would shatter.

Can anyone fucking see me? Please fucking see me. I knew then this was my life now. Let me be hateful, let me be bitter, let me be alone. Fuck it all is what I thought, what I felt. A broken record repeating over and over "you caused this, you failed him, you let him go". Night and day, week after week, month after month, special dates and holidays crept up, yet blindsided me. Especially in the first year, the first year was the hardest. You feel like you're dying inside all again and again. Dragged back to the beginning while kicking, screaming, and fighting to be dragged.

Then those songs, those fucking lyrics, those memories not like gentle waves kissing the shore. But a fucking out-of-control car, pedal pressed to the floor until the wall is hit. It left me ripped open and hemorrhaging inside. I'm still barely surviving, clawing with raw fingers to hold on. Just one more day when before I didn't want to live. I didn't realize grief was slowly unpacking itself into my life. It was pushing me to keep going while torturing me with the loss of you.

Grief early on is never balanced. It swings like a pendulum and goes from one extreme to another depending on what it decides for the day. But as time passes, it becomes more balanced because grief has unpacked its last box and made a home. Grief now inserted into my daily life.

Once grief settled, I was able to learn to stand on my own. I felt like a child learning to walk, to learn to be in a new world without you. I've learned from grief; it was and will always be my teacher. Grief will never leave, it's part of me, it's part of you, it's part of us.

All these years of grief have turned me into a pillar of strength. I've found love again. I've found happiness. I've found the will to live each and every day. I still haven't forgiven myself. I probably never will. But I've learned to become gentle with myself. For now, I can live with that.

Seven years ago I would've never said grief was a gift, but today I can. You were the one that gave me grief. But at the bottom of that grief, I found your love. Your love was and always will still be with me, in my heart, in my new world. I know today you would be proud of how far I have come; for that, I thank you for all you have given me.

there is an ugly side of strength — the side that remains hidden by a mask of endless i am fine the side no one wants to speak of — no one cares if your heart has been ripped out of your chest while it still beats in agony in sinful hands — no matter how many times you bleed crimson contrition — you know you will never be saved is this the time you will not be able to put back the broken pieces — waving your white banner of surrender because even strength has forsaken you — the pain is overwhelming from carrying a lifetime of tragedy which found home deep in your bones, tears being fought back — blurring your vision as you struggle to choke back the catch in your throat — knowing if you speak your tongue will betray you — letting all your secrets escape from the cage of your soul — staining your lips with bittersweet tragedy — strength is not a beautiful gift — strength is terrifying, a constant reminder of how many times you have been broken but still live

the silent treatment is a poison with no antidote

you would never believe who she could become by her submissive demeanor and her soft-spoken voice — she wore those like cheap trinkets of jewelry, little did they know if you were to cross her she became something more; becoming mr. hyde when dr. jekyll does not take his potion she could turn into the most wicked of vixens, ice flowing through her veins, her eyes dark and empty while her tongue turns her words into shrapnel — she is able to destroy you without hesitation leaving you begging for mercy as she walks away in her black leather stilettos beautiful – a word which i still do not comprehend when someone tells me "you are beautiful" "your soul is beautiful" "your scars are beautiful" – how long does it take for someone to comprehend a kind word, a kind gesture – when out of the womb you were treated and told you were the ugliest thing to ever breathe, live, a stain, an atrocity – ingrained in my bones, the words flow through my veins

what is this word called beautiful – i hear so many being called this – but still i cannot comprehend the word still to this fucking day – how am i to believe i am beautiful without the walls of defense to go up – because it is a red flag for me, it means something is wanted, something they want me to give to them – what better way with honeyed lips tinged with lies – to hear beautiful even now makes me cringe

i see beauty in others and yet in the mirror, i do not see an ounce of it in me – i do not feel it in the depths of my soul – i see ugliness imprinted in my dna – i can only see one way and it is to start to believe others about the word beautiful maybe one day i will be comfortable in my skin and believe for once i am beautiful to someone and that someone has to be me

music has become the bandage in healing my wounds

windows down, wind blowing, my tresses swirl, stickiness in the air laced with the smell of salt from the bay, my hand out the window, up and down, up and down until i am in sync with the air current, the hum of the road clears my head, radio turned up, tuning the world out, hypnotized by the full moon as its beams dance on gentle waves, specks of light dot the skyline where they look like fireflies lined up, i close my eyes, memories from my youth replay like a movie but in slow motion, i smile as i am reminded of the times i was wild back when things were simple i know i have been written in stories of others just as i have written of the painful regrets festering wounds, poisonous love a reason why walls are built around hearts, i was fine with placing blame, walking away saying it was not my fault portraying the image of innocence i was the damsel and they were the villain, how i was perfect, they were flawed; i learned the hard way as karma tried to spoon feed it all back to me tenfold; time and again i spit out what was served, refusing to swallow the truth of it all i ran, tried to avoid the blame, the damage i left in my wake of rage wearing the crown of drama queen it took years for me to grow, to finally sit down and feast on the years of karma prepared meals; i learned with each meal i was wrong, i took responsibility in cleaning my plate i begged for forgiveness, some have granted it to me and some have denied me, i have come to the terms for when i was denied i had to forgive myself for me to be better than i was

A HOME NAMED GRIEF

You'll hear "I'm sorry for your loss, I'm here for you". It will play like an old record that has that one groove where the needle gets stuck repeating over and over. You'll give your half-hearted thank you without even knowing you've said it because grief has programmed your brain to give that response.

Behind every thank you is your soul screaming in silent agony. You feel every piece of your heart break, the shards ripping up your insides. You feel you're being hollowed out. You feel like you're dying as you struggle to take the next breath, knowing this is just the beginning.

A new beginning, an excruciating beginning. You try to stand tall, to keep tears from flowing from your already bloodshot eyes. Grief becomes caught in your throat. You try to force a smile with hopes they don't see that grief is feasting on you.

You want to show your strength. How you can be as strong or stronger before grief. Yet you want to scream how the fuck am I to do this? No one ever taught you how to handle grief. It's the hardest lesson to learn, a lifelong lesson.

As the dust begins to settle everyone will walk away from you. They have to, they have their lives to lead. They don't do it with malice. Grief is like that, it isolates, it gives a face to mortality, where it shows death is too real, too close to home. Where it could be their next visitor.

It makes you curse the gods of why do you have to be alone with this gaping hole that no one can see, feel. But yet you want to be alone, trying to make sense of grief.

You'll try to reason with grief, beg grief for just one moment to feel no pain. Your once tall self will be curled up into a ball, holding yourself, trying to forget all this is real. A horrible nightmare you can't wake from. Grief has unpacked its bags. It has found a new home in your surroundings, in you. Your home, your soul becomes a tomb. Grief welcomes visitors that bear the names of solitude, anger, what-ifs, could haves, and ones you never knew even existed.

Every emotion will stake a claim in your new world. It's brutal. You can't just tell them to leave. They're a part of you for the rest of your days. They have sewn themselves to every inch of you. An invisible shroud you can only feel and see.

No matter how hard you fight it, how hard you try to numb yourself grief always knows and shows how you have to feel it. No matter the ugliness it shows. Grief is a teacher in your life now.

In time the pain becomes bearable. It doesn't mean you've moved on. Hell, you never move on. You finally welcome grief and its visitors in your life. You have made a treaty and learn how to live with it every day.

Those bleeding wounds grief has made, no longer bleed out, but trickles now. You're able to stand again, instead of crawl. Every breath isn't as painful as before. Grief will always be there to remind you with a memory, a song, a smell for it to crumble another brick from your world.

But now it's okay, because you know you'll have those moments, those days or hell even weeks. Those times you may feel you're back at the beginning when grief was brand new. Feel those moments, grieve those moments. It's part of your healing, your way to keep moving forward.

You're honoring your grief, your loss because you're still living. You're living for you, you're living for the one you lost, you're living two lives. That's one thing grief can never take away from you.

remember one day all those little things you took for granted — the conversations, laughs, their voice, those pet peeves, i love you's, scribbled love notes, the very sound of their heartbeat — believing it would never end, eventually the day comes when life decides their journey is to be no more — all those things and more will become the biggest part of your life — it will have you on your hands and knees begging the gods to have every little thing back you took for granted — you will be left with memories and photographs you will offer your life, your soul, just to get a glimpse - to breathe it all in and appreciate this time all those little things — i know this because even to this day i still wish for it and miss every little thing i thought would last forever

they created their own universe with a single kiss

it seems like a lifetime ago the time we spent together — endless conversations, laughter and memories made — we mended each other's hearts — playing pool, drinking beers, singing off-key and air guitar — another quarter for the jukebox — glycerine and anybody listening those were our songs — our eyes would lock, our fingers entwined, the world stopped, it was only the two of us, we sang that one lyric the one sung a million times, they one which was our secret way we said i love you "clear, simple and plain"

melancholy comes knocking on my door, bringing along memories — every single time i say not this time but i always tend to answer the door, inviting them in — i try to be polite and accommodating while the pain grows more with every breath and heartbeat

melancholy and memories know the real me, they know they have to remind me they will always be a big part of me — to where i have to feel it and to remember every single detail which haunts me; with no escape, to feel the pain, to taste the salt in my crimson tears, to take my breath away and break my heart all over again

when melancholy and memories decide to take leave i can breathe and feel alive again — but yet it is bittersweet because i know even though i dread their visits, i will miss them until they return again

my love is like whiskey — smooth with a kick of fire

it has been said to heal your bleeding wounds from the past you need to make peace and those wounds will heal but for me, i will never make peace with my wounds for if i did i would be saying goodbye to you and all the memories of us would die — that is something i will never do because those bleeding wounds keep us — keeps me alive i tiptoe on the razor edge, peering into the bottom tempting myself to free fall again – can i fall further than the time before – you see the bottom has become a second home for me – i spiral out of control with hopes to find parts of me i lost – to somehow breathe life back into those tender pieces of me that are now decayed – the pieces no longer fit no matter how hard i try – is this where i am to remain – lost in the darkness with my broken pieces i know i need to get back to the top – but it is always difficult – painful to do alone – i need your help – do you hear me calling your name friend – can you save me

AGONY

It has all seemed hopeless, life and death conspiring for feats your soul has to overcome. Both of them gambling if you can just take one more step, take one more breath.

Ramping up the stakes by beating you down, dragging you through the mud. Leaving you dirtied, bloodied, split wide open with wounds.

Your soul stripped naked and exposed for it to be trampled on. Screams from your blood-stained lips, cursing the gods and their fucking egos.

When will it all end, just let it end. But then you look up as you grasp for that one last thin strand of hope, fate shines brightly. It binds you temporarily with its masterplan, for our grand design to unfold.

I'm not afraid, fate led me to you even though it wasn't the way we wanted it to be. I want to touch your darkness, trace your scars with my bruised fingertips. To hold the shards of your broken heart while tasting the bittersweet pain that lingers on the tip of your tongue.

To hold your hands which are black and blue from beating on the walls as you begged the gods for it all to end. Screaming until your voice is gone, eyes bloodshot and swollen from all the tears you cried alone. Where you held yourself with your own arms.

For the times you've been desperate. Wandering aimlessly through this cold, cruel world. While you waited for just one, just one person who would take you for all you were, all you are, and all you can be. Darlin' there is no more waiting, no more struggling to survive. I'm here by your side and I'm not going anywhere.

Poetry Stained Lips

i dream in monochrome – i search for colors every night, but they elude me like a game of hide and seek – i am always the loser – it is cold, i feel it in my bones – the dreams are always the same – everyone's back is turned from me, leaving me all alone in my dream state – it seems all too real, where i believe i am to wander alone in this world – melancholy and madness make their appearance to let me know i am a ghost in this realm – a mortal shell bound in chains – they assure me they are the only friends – promising me to never leave my side, a pinky swear i reluctantly take because it is better to be a part of something instead of nothing – i walk this dream world road, leaving a trail of crimson tears and bleeding wounds where i will search for colors and hope to find them where the colors will bleed into my waking world she does not believe in quitting and that is why she will conquer the world

i once wasted my time on your honeyed sweet words dripping from your irresistible lips as they were laced with promises, you swore you would always speak the truth — but it was not until i lit the match to all those words you whispered to me — i watched them all burn to ash and it was revealed — all your truths were lies and empty promises just to keep me by your side because you could not bear to be alone with your loneliness and misery

Poetry Stained Lips

she is sunshine and wildflowers — her tresses brushed by the wind — her skin sun-kissed revealing her freckles — the sunlight brought out the green in her eyes — the grass tickled her bare feet she lets out the most intoxicating laugh she dances to the music in her head as she twirls around in her flowing dress — such innocence in the way she moves — plucking dandelions to make wishes — her soul can never be tamed — heaven help the man who falls in love with her

my scars are a road map of all the destinations i have been to but will never revisit

broken dreams and broken heart – pieces fall around me – cutting me deep on the shards of emptiness – leaving imprints of memories stained in blood and agony on the road of life struggling to maintain my grace with one step at a time – searching for a place to call home

Poetry Stained Lips

my demons are subtle at first when they become restless – my ribcage is their prison – they test my bones, looking for a weakness – giving me a twinge of pain here and there, a gasp falls from my lips giving them a taste of freedom – they lead a revolt, clawing and breaking enough bones to escape – leaving chaos in their wake as they run like unruly children – disobeying my pleas to come home – i do not need them inflicting pain with the gnashing of their teeth and razor-sharp claws on the ones i love – even though i am tired of fighting – wanting to breathe a sigh of relief – to feel if even for a moment where i am no longer bound to my demons tonight i will not have to serve myself on a platter for them to feast upon my soul – i have no choice but to bring them back home – back to where they belong – the prison in my bones

TRULY

You truly don't appreciate all those little things. From the pet peeves to having no reason to leave a note except to say I love you until it's all gone. The way you would fall asleep first and your snoring would keep me awake. The nights when we stayed up until dawn watching movies and gorging ourselves on junk food.

Your handheld mine every time we were in the car as we both belted out songs. Our little ones telling us to please stop. The way your eyes lit up every time you looked at me. Telling me I was the most beautiful woman in the world. Those nights when we would lay in bed while reading, my leg thrown across yours.

How you were so proud when you adopted our Boo. Giving her the father she wanted - she needed. The way you held your sons high when they were born. Proud to be a father to three children, our family complete.

When I was diagnosed with my plethora of mental illnesses. You jumped into the fire and cared for me so they wouldn't send me away.

The tears I cried for you as you laid clinging to life, letting you know you couldn't give up the fight.

The night before your surgery as I laid my head upon your chest. Feeling and hearing every single heartbeat, knowing it would be the last time to hear it. A machine would end up pumping your heart with only the sound of parts whooshing in your chest. How I cried with my head on your chest knowing I would never feel or hear your heartbeat again.

Days turned to weeks, then to months where we slept apart. I was in our bed we once shared and you in a lonely hospital room. Our conversations on how to prepare when you came home to spend your remaining months.

The last night I spent with you, wearing blinders because I refused to see the end was near. Getting the call, when I was two minutes away from you, that you took your last breath.

Our children and I standing outside of your room. In shock only to be able to say daddy is gone. Your LVAD machine screeching as the nurse is on the phone getting directions on how to silence it.

I was promised I wouldn't ever have to disconnect the machine which kept you alive. The screeching too much, the nurse didn't understand. I had to disconnect it, even though you were gone, I still feel I cut off your lifeline. When I silenced the machine, I silenced you.

Our oldest unable to walk in, our middle sitting on the couch, our youngest climbing onto your bed, laying his head on your chest with his arms outstretched. Somehow if hugging you would keep you here.

I felt your presence in the room - an unexplainable warmth, like you were trying to calm us and protect us. I don't remember who was there with us, who called, how I drove home. I convinced myself you were just in the hospital and you would be calling me.

Making arrangements that week while every single night I tried to end my life with pills and cocaine. I know today I had gone insane with grief. No one even knew. The day came to say our final goodbye. I said I wasn't going to your funeral, I believed it was a horrible nightmare I couldn't wake up from.

I played the strong hostess. It was all I could do to keep it all together. It wasn't until your eulogy began. All everyone could hear was the sobbing of your oldest son. Right there all our hearts completely broke. Reality set in with the private moment I had with you. Finally crying and begging you please to come back to me. It should've been me not you because you were the best of us both.

Even though every single day we said I love you and how we felt. It still wasn't enough. There was still so much more to be said even though we thought we said it all. With all this, I would do it all over again even with the same results. It may not make sense, but for some who have lost, they will say they understand and do it all again.

Poetry Stained Lips

i used to be ashamed of my pain, my wounds, my scars they reminded me of the times i had no hope, where i thought i would die from them - where i tried to fuck away the pain, to live up to my name of whore, i drank until the veil of darkness would shroud me leaving me to wake with hazy memories, snorting line after line where i could feel alive no matter how short lived or fake it was i believed i was to suffer, i did not understand my pain, my wounds, my scars, i only knew how to receive them, how to wear them, never was i shown how to heal them, to heal me - over the years i had to teach myself on how to heal, how to forgive others not for their benefit but for me to get my footing to become stable - i have slowly learned how to love myself, accept myself, to let go of the things i had no control of and the things i did have control over to know who i was, who i am and who i am striving to become and for me, after it is all said and done i turned my pain, my wounds, my scars into a thing of beauty i feared my breakdowns once until i learned they were leading me to the most beautiful breakthroughs

i have seen music take flight — feeling colors enter my soul — hearing the world speak beckoning me to beauty — while i travel the road of mind-altering experiences opening dimensional doors do you think i love to write about darkness i wish i did not have tragedy in my bones spilling ink has allowed me to keep going reminding me there are others like me who struggle to find light with every breath

at times i envy the wordsmiths who can write about the beautiful parts of love when all i know is pieces that have shattered into razor-sharp shards of melancholy, memories, and madness

will there ever be the day when all my darkness is banished — where i will be able to bask in the warm welcoming light i hold onto hope that one day, someday my dream will be a reality

but until then my words will serve as bandages to heal my bleeding wounds and heart there are times i can only express myself through movie quotes and song lyrics

my rendezvous with 3 a.m. is like lovers meeting in secret to have those few stolen moments of passion while the world slumbers – seducing me with the stillness of the night – unleashing my lust to write from deep within – anticipation builds – breath quickens as my words fall from my parting lips – staining them on parchment in sultry red lipstick quenched in orgasmic bliss the night is my one true friend – we understand each other's darkness

i am tired of wearing a mask – stepping out onto the stage again – having to perform my same role – i have perfected this act all my life – pretending to be something i am not i am a liar – i am a fake because i tell the world i am fine – they applaud and say job well done as my silent screams go unheard

when it is your time – will your final breath be of love or regret

for every time he says i cannot right now i want to – the time is not right – just wait a little longer – one day – she dies more with every word spoken even though she tells him it is fine – how many more words do you think it will take before her heart stops beating – where her love for him which once flourished now chokes and gasps on empty promises – one day it will be a day too late and it is much sooner than you can ever imagine be ready to batten down the hatches for today i am a storm with raging seas

my thoughts race down the tracks like a runaway train again – my chaotic emotions ride as passengers – with held breath – white-knuckled death grip – counting down to see if i can compose a masterpiece to save my sanity – instead, it ends the same way a path of self-destruction ending in a fucking pile of fiery wreckage with no survivors and nothing to be salvaged my eyes are the map to my soul it will be a bittersweet journey of love, loss, hope, and pain – my wounds have scarred will be the compass to guide you – only then you will find me there are times where my heart and mind need a translator to understand each other

do you ever wonder behind those perfectly lined eyes, the tears which have fallen like rain or those perfectly painted lips that quiver to force a smile she catches her breath before she speaks where you cannot hear her voice shake – she wears a mask of beauty instead of revealing the ugliness of her pain where she does not have to explain as if anyone would even look or listen

LOST HEART

Of all the love I have had yours hurt the worst. I felt my heart break, my world crumbled, wanting to cut out the pain. I cursed my heart for loving you with every breath. Time stopped for me; I was going insane.

I do not know how I survived. I just remember crying myself to sleep begging for death to come just so I didn't have to feel. I just wanted to be with you. I was angry when I woke up, I was still here, I was still breathing. A failed attempt; but I wasn't living, I only existed.

Our once home was now a cold tomb; nothing to be touched or moved. It all had to stay the way it was when you were still here. It was my way to hold onto a strand of what remained even though I knew it was gone. You were gone. I slipped in and out of reality. My mind convincing me you would be home at any moment. Just wait, I would tell myself; he will be calling.

I shuffled from room to room trying to find you. Only memories and pictures haunted me. My eyes red and swollen, hair knotted and unbrushed. My body ached just to breathe. I wore the same clothes for days on end; sleep eluded me. I hallucinated, calling out for you with hope you would say, I am here. I was drowning in grief. I was lost without you.

I don't know how long it took to take the first step. The first step to become part of the living world again. It was a learning process to have grief part of my days for the rest of my life. But I know it was you urging me to pick up the pieces even if it meant cutting me deep; leaving me wounded and bleeding to piece myself back together again.

I had to let the pain wash over me, the blood to seep through every part of me, and my tears to cleanse me. I had to dig down deep to pull it all together not just for me, but for you, for us. I had to give you back life even if it was with my heartbeat and breath. I had to live if I was to honor you. To prove death doesn't have a hold on love. Death cannot destroy love. Death can only separate us temporarily but that is all it can do.

When my last breath is taken, freeing me from this mortal shell, I know I will find you among the stars greeting me with open arms. Until then I will live, I will love, I will breathe not just for me, but for you.

Poetry Stained Lips

Poetry Stained Lips

INTENSITY

do you know how to slay the what-ifs, pain, and heartbreak — you slay them with the spilled ink from your veins

i am not a picture book for you to casually flip through pretty pages — i am tattered and worn, full of twists and turns, filled with layers of detail — my soul has filled volumes of half-finished stories — you will become lost at times searching for answers in my footnotes like breadcrumbs left to guide your way — absorbing every single word through your fingertips — coursing through your veins — taking your breath away as you become part of my pages, a part of my story, a part of me

our photographs captured our once perfect moments with just a simple click – memories frozen in time imprinted on fragile paper which now sit in a box collecting dust – the seasons have changed and years have passed – our photographs of us begin to fade, the corners now bent and frayed – once vibrant colors have become dull, no matter how many grains of sand have slipped away in the hourglass of life – when melancholy calls i cannot resist visiting the past, searching for the person i was when i was with you, the memories wash over me until it feels like it was yesterday i have walked through fire time after time where the flames now bow in my presence

they deemed me unworthy — they convinced me to walk on eggshells to silence my voice while keeping to the shadows — i finally realized their view was skewed, i knew i was worth — from that day forward i stepped into the light — no longer a shrinking violet every step i took shook the ground and every word i gave breath to became a roar

Poetry Stained Lips

i have ripped my heart out of my chest a thousand times
and each time i have picked up the pieces, gently
bandaging them – placing them back into my chest –
sewing it all up with tears, regrets, and what-ifs until my
fingers bleed the pain will ease until the heaviness
returns, raging to be released, it feels like my bones are
being crushed to dirty grittiness splitting open my scars
to bleed crimson attrition – leaving every inch of me
battered and bruised – bringing me to my knees
screaming in agony – knowing the only way to survive is
to rip my chest back open like i have done a thousand
times before just to breathe even if it is a single breath

he stood on the railroad tracks just to be a part of her train wreck world

she only stood out in a crowd because those circles and cliques made her stand out – with the pointing of fingers and whispers even though they did not know her – they made their assumptions snubbing their noses at her because she was not a cookie-cutter image of them – it used to bother her that she was not accepted but as she got older and wiser she realized it was better to be alone and true to herself and not a part of mask-wearing charlatans

AWKWARD

As a child, I was awkward and shy. Where even being around my classmates left me in a state of panic. Back then it wasn't called anxiety, it was just called being nervous. I was told I would grow out of it.

In my youth, I had a small circle of friends, but I never truly fit in. I would withdraw into myself for weeks, months often losing friends because I came across as cold and not caring. It wasn't there or my fault, we were young, and we didn't understand why I was this way.

As a young adult in the workforce, you wouldn't even know I even existed. Again, a few friends but I still felt out of place. It wasn't until much later I realized the way I felt and responded was due to a shitty childhood and to mental illness.

When I worked my way up from a clerk to working in a sales office I became a social butterfly to an extent, but still a wallflower. I always tried hard, but I could never pull it off, being me.

With my hubby, he made it all feel natural. We had date nights, outings with the kids, mini-vacations. We were always busy and on the go. It was the only time I felt comfortable in my own skin. I felt alive and free from anxiety. Then it all changed when he had an incurable medical condition. Our busy days out consisted of us traveling to doctor appointments or visiting him when he was in the hospital.

As time passed we became more and more homebound. Which for me became like a warm blanket giving me comfort because I had all I wanted and needed in the arms of him in our home. I didn't miss going out and doing things. I wanted to be within the four walls of a house full of love as our time together ticked away loudly.

After he passed, I thought I could go back to being social. I tried and got a part-time job just to interact with others. The feeling was short-lived because now every time I had to leave the house I was filled with anxiety. A turn of events with my youngest child made it easy to leave my job. I was back I felt like I belonged, feeling safe and as if I could shut out the world like turning off a tv.

I do get out some. If my kids want to go places, I'll go. I even have it down to three days a month to pay bills, run errands, and grocery shop for the month. Each month I think of every possible scenario and all the horrible things that could go wrong, but of course, they didn't. I dread those times and breathe a sigh of relief when it's all over.

I know many will say I'm missing out on all the beauty this world has. But I have also missed out on all the ugliness. Will I ever be transformed from caterpillar to social butterfly? I'm in love with my solitude, my four walls, my own little world. But who knows, maybe one day I'll fly on brand new wings.

if you are brave enough to search for my beauty beneath all the layers of ugliness you will first need to journey to find the way to revive my shattered heart that waits for love and understanding — it will be a treacherous road to travel, you will need to use my scars which adorn my flesh as a compass to guide you — you will need to tenderly trace each scar with your fingertips, to learn of their secrets their stories — how they once burned when they were cavernous wounds, bleeding out crimson contrition, begging to be saved — only then you will be able to find me, maybe then you will be able to love me and see the beauty of my scars

she disguised her demons by wearing a mask of a goddess

like pandora i opened my box – unleashing hell upon my world – i struggled with my demons – fighting to lock them away only to find all along the one thing i needed was at the bottom – it was hope – hope was waiting – hope had always been there – hope was all i needed to prevail do you ever feel like you are living in two different worlds – where you fall to your knees because you do not have the fight in you today – tired of keeping love and grief separated – you know what comes next so you will make yourself as small as you can by holding yourself tight with hopes this time when your two worlds collide, your heart will not explode into a tragic supernova – but you have been here before – yet it seems brand new because wounds begin to bleed, to allow the memories to come flooding back – the crashing waves of the past and present wash over you until you are unable to catch your breath – you try to tread through it, but you know you have to submit – allowing love, grief, past and present to balance your two worlds again your name plays on repeat with every heartbeat

darlin' i know of the others — the ones who did not care for you — the ones who tossed you aside instead of delving into your soul — the ones who only saw you as a dust jacket of words they thought were meaningless — but i am here now to take you down from the shelf, dusting you off, running my fingers down your spine breathing you in as i open you — i trace every one of your words ever stained in ink on the parchment of your soul — losing myself in your pages, never wanting your story to end, for me to be a part of it — i know how you are a beautiful masterpiece, a masterpiece i was meant to discover

it is rare but there are times where she wants it to be all about her – do not tell her she is selfish do not tell her a strong woman does not need to have the spotlight – she needs to shine every now and then – let her take the stage – getting a standing ovation with the roar of an encore, encore as she takes her bow – she has stood in the shadows far too long – giving her heart and soul at times she has been wounded just so others could chase their dreams – they know she is always there to catch them when they fall – but who is there to catch her when she falls – no one, no one at all – she always has to pick herself up like she has a thousand times before – wiping away the blood and tears – forcing a smile as she wishes someone would sacrifice the way she has – for once – just one time she wants it to be about her

SMILES DISAPPEAR

I have noticed through photographs our smiles have disappeared. Yes, you may look at my face and the faces of my children and see smiles. But what you don't see is the sadness in the eyes. Only a few can really see deep within the eyes of the photographs, into our souls seeing the sadness, loss, pain, and grief.

I didn't notice it until recently when I was scrolling through my online photo albums. I started to compare before 2011 and after 2011.

Before 2011 each of us had a natural smile, a twinkle in the eyes just like him. He gave us that happiness and smiles for the love he had for us and the love we had as a family.

Then the fateful day of November 1, 2011, the twinkle in our eyes faded and died with him. Our hearts broke and every smile after that has been a mask worn to cover the grief felt with every heartbeat.

I can't believe I was blinded by it. Maybe it was because I wanted to believe we were happy again. We had come so far in picking up the pieces, learning and living with the grief in every breath.

It's the moments we will never have that made our smiles fade with every passing day. He was the reason behind our smiles in photographs and in life. He was our breath of fresh air and full of life. We were as others were drawn to him.

Will the day ever come when I look at our photographs and see the twinkle in our eyes again and the real smiles return? Or are those days forever gone and a mask will always be carried to smile on cue, hiding the grief, when that photograph is taken?

she was exquisite in the way she wore her tragedies

she drops to her knees – screaming in agony – the last of her adrenaline running through her veins as she rips the rest of the broken pieces of her heart from her chest tears of crimson contrition stain her cheeks – cursing and begging the gods to release her from a lifetime bondage of tragedy – she knows her pleas will not be heart – the only way she can save her sanity – to quell the madness, to stop the demons from tearing at her tender flesh – a fire cleansing from her funeral pyre, her sins ignite – burning away the anguish longed buried in her bones – maybe this time baptism by fire will transcend her to the inner peace she desires fear came knocking on my door again even though i removed the welcome mat i still answered the door for it annoyed me but piqued my interest what fear was bringing me this time; fear rushed by me pushing me aside, setting down at my table spreading it all out like a grand feast to be had my eyes grew big and panic began to settle in i knew i still was full of fear's last meal, but fear was quite the fast talker and what it was offering melted like butter, dazzling my senses fear ripped open my soul serving it on a platter maybe this time it will not be as bad coaxing me to take a bite along with another and another - fear began to consume me - just a little more - fear held the fork to my lips - pleasure with each morsel force fed - scenarios still fresh on my tongue - i tried to chew and swallow - more and more until i started to choke - i spewed it all out back in fear's face - this time i refused to gorge on fear's feast - excusing myself from the table - i showed fear the door, slamming it shut - only to hear fear whisper - darlin' i will be back soon to feed you more

sinful lips beg with quickened breath to feel your wickedness

you tell me to breathe, just breathe, like it is a simple thing to do — but darlin' what you do not realize is i have been trying to breathe, just breathe my entire life — it may not be today or tomorrow, but one day, someday, i will be able to show you i can breathe, just breathe

Poetry Stained Lips

i have played with my madness like a cat and mouse game over the years, putting on my mask taking the role of the muse of tragedy — only for it to find me time and time again to reclaim its cold, harsh grip on my reality i have tried to reason with madness to call a truce, hell i have even danced on the line between living and death just to find a moment of peace; i did not know i had to learn from my madness to taste the sweat of bitterness on my tongue, choking on it like acrid smoke, letting my throat burn as i spewed out the ashes, blackening my blood-stained lips, freeing it from its bonds — i embrace it, feed it the love it had been starving for i could no longer douse my madness in my pain and lighting it up with rage to watch it all burn, trying to convince myself it will all be okay it needed to be nurtured and shown the way, to not be like an out-of-control child full of tantrums; through it all i finally have accepted my madness, it will always be a part of me, it will be a fine line to walk as long as there is breath in me; but at least for now my madness slumbers there are times i look in the mirror and it is like two strangers are meeting

i know how you hate to break — you think if you break then you have failed — no darlin' that is far from the truth — there is strength in breaking you have to break at times before you can take the next step — breaking is like a trust fall — you will be a little scare — unsure of yourself — it needs to be done — i know this to be true because darlin' i have been where you are now — so close your eyes take a deep breath and trust darlin'….trust and fall

ANGRY

Another day closer to when I lost you. At times it feels like it was yesterday. My chest hurts, my heart pounds, anxiety fills my throat as I choke on the words I need to get out.

Tears will fall at the very thought of you. I am force-fed memories; at times it's too much to digest. My head convinces me all of it – us - was pure perfection.

When you took your last breath, death skewed my reality giving me a false sense of peace; attempting to ease my suffering, but pain twists its knife of regrets and what-ifs.

I pound my fist against the wall trying to make sense of it all. Have all my past transgressions come back tenfold to teach me this was the consequence?

Grief gnashes its teeth into my open wounds to keep them bleeding; where they will never heal or scar.

Even after all these years, there is nothing beautiful about me losing you. I walk through this world speaking of how you travel among the stars.

How much more bullshit do I need to convince myself you are in a better place? When in reality I have no fucking clue if I will ever see you when my last breath is taken.

How can I keep that glimmer of hope alive, wishing I will be with you one day?

But all I see is how death and grief are cruel, cold, and calculating. The perfect couple as they feed off the souls of those left behind.

Does this make me angry? Damn right it does.

Poetry Stained Lips

one day you will miss her — it will hit you out of nowhere — you will think back to all those times she sent you texts, songs she claimed as hers, poems she wrote for you, about you — her voice when she said i love you, her laugh, and the way she wanted you

you will drop to your knees cursing the gods when you know you were to blame all the little things you thought were insignificant was in reality who she was

you let her go without telling her all those things you were afraid to say you put up your walls before she could wound you, even though she never did you did not want to risk your heart all because you had been hurt before

in the end, you destroyed her when all she wanted was to be by your side you realize you should have just taken the chance to believe in yourself, to believe in her, to believe in love but instead you were afraid and you lost it all the beginning to our end started when your betrayal covered my skin in filth — carving pain into my bones

pain has been my intimate consort for as long as i can remember — the foundation i have built my life upon — pain has never abandoned me it has saved me by coursing through my veins my tragedies have wrapped around me like a warm blanket — giving me comfort — security as i bleed tragedies out onto paper over and over — i do fear a day will arrive — my pain stripped away — but by then it will not matter i will be nothing but bare-bones and an empty shell — crushed into dust

Poetry Stained Lips

i hate the skin i am in
my soul feels bruised
my bones brittle from all
the pain carved on them
i fight back tears
i tell myself do not do it
do not let them flow
it is a sign of weakness
i bite my bottom lip hard
until it is swollen
colors of blues and purples
glistening with crimson
i take the back of my hand
smearing it across my lips
as if i were trying to wipe
away all traces of a bitter kiss
i was forced to wear on my lips
the words i have swallowed are
regurgitated until they fill my throat
with the stickiness of filth and shame
i taste it on my tongue but i am unable
to purge the melancholy and madness
i can only sit in silence as it devours
me until i become an empty shell

in today's world hate is easier to find than love – we need to bury the hate and resurrect the love

i used to want to hear the once upon a time where the prince saves the princess and they live happily ever after fairy tale – but i no longer desire them – i want to hear about how the warrior queen who is the first to unsheathe her sword on the battlefield – war paint covering her body as she puts fear in the hearts of her enemies with her warrior scream – no hesitation – ready to shed blood even if it is hers – to seize what she has always wanted – the sweet taste of victory of doing it all by her own accord

Poetry Stained Lips

pretty little thing caressed by my fingertips, how you let me know this time is an exception to the rule, the one i am not supposed to break i am going to argue the points on why i should not but i already know it will all be one-sided; you are just here to tantalize my senses, promising me to take me to the place where i will not loathe myself even if it is just another one of your fucking lies, the voice inside my head sounds like a skipped part of a record, where the needle never avoids repeating over and over, do it, do it, do it, do it to feel fucking something, anything; with eyes closed, you end up on the tip of my tongue waiting to be swallowed to begin your torturous pleasure sweetness is what i desire, but i know you can only offer a bitter taste, melting, sliding down my throat like honey for me not to gag on your façade that i need you, want you; you get what you want as i submit to you, i may have lost this battle, but in the end i will win the war

TEARS

I was brought up being told crying was a weakness. I was also told crying was a sign of guilt for something even if I didn't do anything wrong. I was told to toughen up, to lock away all those tears and emotions. For years I tried to train myself not to feel; just because others wanted me this way.

It's selfish and cruel for someone to do this to a person especially when you're an empath. It's just impossible to do. Just because they are that way and think it's the right way. It's not. It has taken me a lifetime and another day to undo the damage of the words, "don't cry, you're weak." Those words I still can't abide to.

Yes, I've held back the tears until they reach the top of the spillway of the dam walls I've put up. Yes, I still hear the words resonate, "don't cry", as I feel the catch in my throat, my eyes well up, making it too blurry to see. I can taste the saltiness on my lips as the tears begin to fall.

I'll still try to fight the urge, to stand strong. But there are times when the tears will spill onto the ground in front of you. It doesn't happen often; it shocks others when I do because they have always seen a pillar of strength no matter my tragedies.

Poetry Stained Lips

But if I cry in front of you, being able to stand in front of you, with my soul naked and vulnerable, it's a sign of how I trust you with every part of me. I know you won't give me pity, but the reassurance it will all be okay.

And with these words, I'll keep reminding myself it's okay to cry. I'll let my tears wash over me, cleansing my soul. But most importantly I'll shut out those words of "don't cry, you're weak", because I'm not weak and sometimes strength is shed through tears.

the ones who get angry at you when you speak your truths are usually the first ones to call you a liar

my words begin as a sugary sweetness on the tip of my tongue waiting for me to breathe life into them – they fall from my lips – losing their sweetness like they have a thousand times before igniting into a firestorm – the air is heavy with the remnants of brimstone – my words gasp for breath – struggling clawing their way to bleed onto parchment coveting to be immortalized but like their brethren before them, they end up dirtied and blackened as they suffocate to their demise grief is not affected by time for the living the ones left behind, the rawness and sting of a wound which will never heal, never scar grief is a bit of a diva and never stands in the shadows for long — it is always there to remind me of the day it came and unpacked itself in my life, it has left bits of haze and grey fading the once vibrant colors in my world it rips out memories with a smell, a sound, a feeling to bring me to my knees — the taste of bitterness grief has placed on my tongue never able to swallow it whole, grief force feeds me bits and pieces, even to this day i choke on it — a tsunami of what-ifs, could have beens, should have beens; destroying the walls i have built - grief takes control leaving me helpless to tread in a sea of emotions and tears — at times i wish i could drown; my battle with grief is a lost cause, it drains my strength, and makes me weak — i am unable to be the rock everyone expects me to be; i now submit and let grief rule me — i have become grief broken heart, shattered dreams rip open my flesh - salty tears sting as they drown in my cavernous wounds of love's illusion

the only dance i held closest to my heart was the one i had with death – elegant graceful – all my melancholy memories turned into music as death held me close his icy grip warmed me – i waited for his kiss – instead, he bowed as the music faded – vowing it was not my time but a mere taste to linger on my lips

Poetry Stained Lips

it is difficult to get through the days let alone the nights – the night only brings solitude mixed with tears, regrets, and what-ifs conquering the world will have to wait like it always does – grief is in the driver seat for now – pressing the pedal down to the floor – fishtailing down the road – crashing head-on into the brick wall of depression from the wreckage my chest is crushed my heart bruised and scars ripped open time is my foe – pain is still my teacher everything is felt tenfold – i would like a pause button – even if for a moment – to breathe and not feel fucking anything i have saved my soul from being poisoned by swallowing the antidote named forgiveness

love letters written in the sand under the stars which cling to the black velvet sky – the ebb and flow of gentle waves slowly erase my words of love – carrying my message upon their crest the wind blows through my tresses – the smell of salt air puts me in a trance – closing my eyes i make a wish will this be the night your soul will be out there to catch my love before the moon kisses the ocean farewell

<u>11/1/2018</u>

Grief isn't affected by time for the living; the ones left behind. The rawness and sting of a wound that will never heal, never scar.

Grief is a bit of a diva and never stands in the shadows for long. It is always there to remind me of the day it came and unpacked itself in my life.

It has left bits of haze and grey fading the once vibrant colors in my world. It rips out memories with a smell, a sound, a feeling to bring me to my knees.

The taste of bitterness grief has placed on my tongue. Never able to swallow it whole. Grief force-feeds me bits and pieces; even to this day I choke on it.

A tsunami of what-ifs, could have beens, should have beens destroying the walls I have built. Grief takes control, leaving me helpless to tread in a sea of emotions and tears. At times I wish I could drown.

My battle with grief is a lost cause. It drains my strength making me weak. I'm unable to be the rock everyone expects me to be. Now I will submit and let grief rule me.

I have become grief.

my heart is heavy tonight – it aches as i try to keep my tears behind my mask – fighting back the trembling in my voice as we speak over the telephone – needing to be strong for the both of us – if i saw you right now i would crumble – how do you let go of someone you love with all your heart – when everything is perfect with what we have – but knowing it needs to be done for you to find yourself – find your inner peach – we are no longer enough to have happiness – stolen moments will be shelved – melancholy memories collecting dust – a fork in the road where our paths will make us part – i know you love me and i love you – maybe this was all we were supposed to have – just a glimpse – a moment – a pause in life until fate determines what is to come next our hearts will be broken – cutting us deep – wounds bleeding – only time will be able to heal us – i know i will always carry you in my heart – sometimes love cannot conquer all – sometimes love is not enough you will need to learn to speak the language of my soul if you want to hear its whispers between the beats of my heart

bestie (best-ie) — the one who never sugarcoats the truth, calls you out on your bullshit; the inside jokes, laughs until your side hurts, 2 a.m. call when it has all fallen apart, never letting you stand alone, picks you up when you fall, a pillar of strength, courage of a warrior; star-dust in the veins, a heart that beats fire, a spine of steel; reminds you of who the fuck you are, raises you up and straightens your crown, unbreakable soul bond, knows all your hopes, fears, and dreams, pinky promises, falling star wishes, i swear, i promise, cross my heart pacts, you got me and i got you always and forever person he loaded up the bullets — waving his love gun carelessly — to release his load into any woman who falls for his charms — the thrill of the hunt the euphoric high — a notch upon his belt to make him feel alive — never letting them know he has a woman he hides in the shadows — she is the one who is by his side day in and day out always has his back — she fights for his love and attention — she dies a little more every day as he turns to another — she will never give up on him — she sees past his pain — cynicism — the hate he has for himself — she still believes he can be saved — she knows she is just a standby runner up — consolation prize — 2 a.m. drunk call a night when his ego is hungry — needing to be fed — she will never leave until he takes that final aim — the kill shot to break her heart — her spirit to — to destroy her notions of love

if overthinking was a sin - i would be damned for all eternity

i have stood in the shadows of others far too long where i have deprived myself - understand when i wish you the best as we part ways — a new journey awaits me — this new beginning will be about me and for me — this is my time to blossom

Poetry Stained Lips

and sometimes i wonder who we would be with the pain we carry in our hearts eyes diverted to the ground where no one could see how the heart bleeds, searching for empathy even if it is from a stranger instead i take the bleeding parts of my heart, the tourniquet that can no longer hold the broken pieces into place, i put those pieces in my pockets like breadcrumbs fed to birds; but instead, i scatter those bleeding pieces as i walk this lonely road hoping someone will stop me, grab my hand, carrying my pieces until they are healed, but it will never happen because no one fucking cares anymore

DECADE OF TRUTHS

I've been sitting here thinking of these last ten years and can't believe I've made it through.

Ten years ago, my Christopher was still with us. Little did we know within six months he would be told he was terminal. Time was no longer on our side, hell it was never on our side. We welcomed our first grandson in 2011. I knew Christopher stayed until he was born. Our first grandchild would be the only one he would ever hold.

I became a widow and my will to live disappeared. I self-medicated and when it wasn't enough to numb the pain. The handful of pills taken was the next step for me. I didn't want to live in a world without Christopher.

Little did I know my attempt would fail. I began to self-medicate, popping pill after pill, snorting line after line of coke. Taking everything and anything to numb the pain. Nothing mattered. My grief made me insane, I see that now.

I don't know how I made it through that time. But I did, I realized I was meant to be here. My life was not over. I had to pick myself up, to keep going because I had three children who looked to me for the answers.

I was now the head of our household. I was the one to raise our children. I was the one to hold their hand, wipe their tears, love them with all I had, to show them we have to keep going. To be an example that no matter what life gives us, we have to keep living.

My children were lost in a sea of emotions. Too young to grasp the concept of grief. They clung to me and looked to me to take away their pain. They begged me to bring their daddy back to them. I heard a million and one times how it was unfair.

They blamed me for Christopher not being here. How could they not. I blamed myself for it too. Maybe if I would've done more, been more, Christopher would still be here. But grief does that in the beginning, it knows the wound is fresh. It finds a way to cast blame on the one who would take it and carry it.

Then our lives changed again. I found something I swore I never would want again. I swore I was going to be the grieving widow, wearing black, alone for the rest of my days. But fate stepped in and I fell in love.

I fell in love with a man who I knew only as a friend. I wasn't looking and neither was he. But knowing my Christopher he had his hand in this. Christopher loved us both with all his heart and must have known we would be great together even before we knew it. This man has made my children and grandchildren as his own. To this day we're still together.

Poetry Stained Lips

There were still ups and downs not just from the grief and learning to live with it every day. But I still battled daily with my mental illnesses. It took all my strength on some days just to breathe. I only had one slip where I had planned my suicide. To end it once and for all. I reached out with a vague post and only one person heard my cry. That person saved my life by just listening to me. It was the last time I ever considered suicide.

As time with grief made itself a home in my life. My best friend of over twenty years helped me through so much. She was a young widow, but further out than me. She comforted me, she advised me, she assured me I wasn't crazy for all I was feeling, thinking. She told me there would come a day, I would be doing what she was doing for me. I scoffed at her, telling her she was crazy. I have since told her she was absolutely right, and I understood as widows we need to be there for other widows. To help them, to let them know they don't walk alone with grief and loss.

That day came, a young woman I met through social media. A young woman who lost her husband too soon. We bonded over our grief. Now I was the one to be there to comfort, advise and assure her. To this day she is my best friend and writing partner as well.

I began to write, at first, it was a diary. Hidden from the world, not willing to share it with anyone. I then started to try my hand at poetry. Believe me, it wasn't pretty. Even after all these years reading them, I cringe when I read it. But I see where I was trying to pour emotions out even if they came out not making sense to no one but me.

We started a writing page on social media; eventually, we wrote our first book and published it. We hoped it would help others grieving a light. The next year I published my longer writings, the year after another book of poetry.

Along the way, I went from crawling on bloodied hands and knees to learning to walk, to standing on my own. I found strength; my spine became steel. I can honestly say the last few years, I've started to heal in more than one aspect of my life. I never thought it would be possible, but it was happening.

I cut ties with my mother finally. It was hard to do, but she was just as toxic as my father. I finally accepted they didn't deserve me. They didn't deserve to be part of my life ever again. I felt a huge weight was finally lifted. The little girl in me was finally able to breathe without fear of consequence. I feel like this past year I've been able to start my healing from childhood trauma. I may have to heal the rest of my life. Yes, it will be messy at times. I'm ready for it to be messy, because I have control over me, my healing, and the love i'm beginning to give myself.

The years, this past decade, has passed quickly, yet it hasn't – birthdays, holidays, anniversaries, celebrations. Between all of those there were and will always be breakdowns, tears, regret, and what-ifs. Grief still knows how to pick at the wound we learned to live with every single day. But I'm learning to make those breakdowns less by remembering the good times, the laughs, the memories.

I know one thing is for certain I'm growing, I'm thriving. My children are growing, they are thriving. My daughter, who was 16 when she lost her father, now 24, married to her soulmate and blessed with three little boys. My boys, who were 8 and 5, now 16 and 13 are growing to be great men. I'm proud I'm not screwing it all up even though at times I feel like I am. I'm not perfect, but I'm trying and will always try. I will never and can never quit.

This decade has been one hell of a trip, but through it all I know I'm not just stronger, but my children are too.

I got this. We got this.

is it ever going to matter to any one of those nights she could not sleep where she held herself as she cried until she could barely breathe

is it ever going to matter to any one of those times she sat with her finger lingering over the send button, then deleted it because she did not want to be a burden

is it ever going to matter to any one of those days when she grips the pen waiting for her veins to open up and bleed onto paper trying to find the words to save her sanity

is it ever going to matter to anyone at all – one day it will but by then it will be filled with regrets and what-ifs of words left unsaid – love undeclared as memories will be the only thing that remains and even then those will be a fleeting thought

Poetry Stained Lips

i am not a victim when battles are lost - i am still a warrior who will win the war

i was blinded by your charm — your wit - your devilish grin — unable to see the poison you slipped past me — you allowed me to drink to what i thought would be forever instead it was love's bittersweet demise when my words fail to flow – where my ink in my veins has run dry – my pain has made me numb you will ask me what is wrong – my words will die upon my lips before they are even given life to live i am unable to articulate one single syllable as my tears begin to flow like a river thawing on the first day of spring – i will choke on the lump in my throat unable to swallow – i will only be able to give you a song to play or a poem to read by someone who was able to bleed their pain – their words at times feel as if they were ripped from my chest – it is their words which can relate to every single tear i cry – every beat of my heart, the breaths i take, their words paint my pain into a beautiful masterpiece with their soul-soothing voice and the stroke of their pen without me uttering a word – my pain is elucidated my strength blossomed by consuming the softness in me cultivating a spine of steel

one day my past and present will meet at a fork in the road — they will have to decide if they are to part ways or to embrace each other — making amends and begin a new journey as one

another day closer of when i lost you, at times it feels like it was yesterday; my chest hurts, my heart pounding, anxiety fills my throat as i choke on the words i need to get out, tears well and fall at the very thought of you; i am force fed memories; at times it is too much to digest as my head convinces me all of it, us, was pure perfection; it was far from it, it only became perfection when you took your last breath; death will skew reality to give you a false sense of peace, to attempt to ease the suffering; but pain twists its knife of regrets and what-ifs; i pound my fists against the wall to try to make sense of it all, has all my past transgressions come back tenfold to teach me this was the consequence grief gnashes its teeth into my open wounds to keep them bleeding where they will never be able to heal and scar; even after all these years there is nothing beautiful about me losing you; i walk through this world speaking of how you travel among the stars, how much more bullshit do i try to convince myself that you are in a better place when in reality i have no fucking clue or even if i will see you when i take my last breath; how can i keep that glimmer of hope alive, wishing i will be with you one day; but all i see is how death and grief are cruel, cold and calculating, the perfect couple as they feed off the souls of those left behind; does all this make me angry, damn right it does

GRIEF WRAPPED CHRISTMAS

Nine years ago I was trying to prepare myself and our kiddos, to get through the first Christmas without Christopher. It had only been 53 days since he passed away. How was I going to do this?

Christmas was Christopher's time — he loved to decorate, he played Christmas music non-stop on repeat, enjoy hot chocolate while driving us around to look at Christmas lights, and he picked out those perfect gifts and wrapped them with love and care.

He became a little boy again during this time. His eyes wide and twinkled, barely able to contain his excitement. He was the kind of person that if you said "bah humbug" he would win you over and have you believe again in the spirit of Christmas.

When he was healthy, he decorated our house inside and out. The outside was covered in lights, from the roof, awning, trees, and bushes. You name it, if lights could go on it, lights went on it. Our house would look like the house from the Christmas Vacation movie.

Christopher would spend hours getting it all perfect. He would be up early in the morning and put the finishing touches into the night. Without fail he would climb up and down the ladder. Hearing the sound of the staple gun almost became a melody.

Every single year I would catch out of the corner of my eye and hear him roll off the roof onto the bushes or falling out of the tree because he got tangled in the very lights he was hanging. He would get up, say I'm good, and get back to it.

The first Christmas was cold and dark. It was painful to even look at anything resembling Christmas. Christopher was

Christmas and now he was gone. The loss of him was unbearable. The spirit of Christmas died with him.

I know I overcompensated that very first Christmas without him. I bought the kiddos everything they asked for and more. I believed if I gave them enough, somehow it would help with our grief. Maybe it would fill this gaping hole that grief had made. I threw money at grief as if I was trying to bribe it to be gentle with us; to go away.

I wasn't sure how I was going to make it. I barely functioned, breathing was excruciating. No one told me that grief is messy. Grief would come in all forms — a smell, a song, a picture, a memory, a holiday, a commercial, a special date. Grief is a trickster and you never know when you'll be knocked down and counted out.

As I was falling apart, there was one person picking up my pieces. I'm grateful for my best friend. She was a young widow with small kids just like me. She was a few more years out than me with widowhood. She has always been my rock and she was wise when it came to firsts because she already lived it, experienced it, survived it.

Without me even asking she came over because she knew how hard it would be for that first Christmas. She could hear my voice tremble and how I was overwhelmed. We wrapped present after present. We talked some and then there were times we wrapped presents in silence.

She was my calm when I was the raging storm. She brought sanity and peace during this time. She carried me through all these firsts and more. She gave me strength to keep going. Even though our Christmases aren't what they used to be, we still celebrate. She was the one who brought the spirit of Christmas back to life for us.

Even though Christopher will be gone for nine Christmases, it's still a difficult time. The grief will always be there. It never gets easier; we just learn how to have it in our everyday lives. Some days will be good, and some days will be soul-crushing. The ones we have lost too soon are always with us. Remember to be gentle with yourself and breathe. You will make it through.

it is said home is where the heart is, but they never say home can be a tomb when your heart has been broken

love can live forever or love can die in an instance – the fate of it lies with the double-edged sword – will it remain sheathed or will it be wielded

Poetry Stained Lips

i opened the doors to the sanctuary of my heart — i could see you were weary from life — i could see the light in your eyes had dimmed — i invited you in with no strings attached — i just wanted to tend to your bleeding wounds to wipe away your pain to give you love and hope — i wanted to be your light as you walked through your darkness — instead, you wiped your dirty feet on my heart making it impure — you took the sanctuary of my heart and shattered it — leaving me all but one piece where i would never be whole — you walked away with that piece — notching it upon your belt like a trinket — it was a prize for you just like the other sanctuary of hearts you devastated before me you may feel at times hope has forsaken you but it has not — it is always with you even if it is just a glimmer

i wonder if hurtful words appeared on the flesh displayed for all the world to see, would people become compassionate or would it become a competition on who has the most wounds and scars

Poetry Stained Lips

my heart is heavy – my mind is clouded – i am crying crimson tears but my soul has clarity – the sadness overwhelms me of how i should fight this battle all alone – to bring heartache and worry to all i love seems selfish on my part – i should have sewn my lips shut and worn the mask reciting my perfect line of i am fine – instead i drug you all into this war with me – on the battlefield of my enemy without thinking ahead of how many of you will be wounded every time life strikes me – leaving me more wounded – please understand if i have made your heart heavy – it was never my intent i just did not want to be alone – i thought having you all by my side in battle was for love, hope and strength – not for me to tend to the wounds i inflicted on your tender souls – even though i know all of you would bleed for me as i have for you – i am sorry and beg for your forgiveness i can write a million different ways of how i love you but until my soul kisses yours only then you will feel love's intensity

darkness has taken hold – pulling my heartstrings until a haunting symphony is birthed from my despair – hypnotizing me – leading me to be enveloped in the cloak folds of melancholy and madness

I GOT DRESSED TODAY

What may be a simple task for many, is at times impossible for others. You want to explain or give reasons of why you just can't. You silently hope it will be a red flag for someone to ask. Instead, you keep those words that taste like filth trapped in your throat. You desperately keep silent in the same clothes you've had on for what seems like forever.

You can't even bear to look in the mirror. If you do catch a glimpse of your reflection it's of someone you don't even recognize. Your stomach is tied in knots making food repulsive. You gag at the very thought of it. You block out all light, darkness becomes a cloak. Then the thought of taking a shower to wash off all the pain is impossible. You know how the water and soap will be excruciating to your skin. How it hurts with every bead of water, every bubble of soap. It feels as if your skin is on fire and will be scarred. You don't brush your hair and let it knot because when you do every hair follicle screams in agony and comes out in clumps.

Your lips become sharp like a razor from dehydration. Your eyes red, swollen from crying with a shade of black beneath them to highlight them better. Your sleeping pattern is fucked — you sleep all day only to wander the halls at night battling your demons. Your nightmares have come to life. It makes you feel more disgusted – feeling unworthy to draw your next breath. It feels as if time has stopped. The only sound is your heartbeat pounding in your chest, in your ears. You feel like you're going slowly insane. The ugly parts now have taken over, dragging you deeper in the pit of despair and darkness. Self-care is now non-existent because it's too painful. You let it fall to the wayside another day.

You want a release from the chains that have you bound. You beg please give me the strength. But you know your begging will always go unanswered. You sift through all your mistakes, your what-ifs, your incoherent thoughts. You struggle to make mental notes of I'll do it all tomorrow when it's a new day. Because tomorrow has to be better, tomorrow is the day. Right? Tomorrow will be the day you'll conquer the world, Right? Until then, you take a deep breath while clinging to a single strand of hope that tomorrow will be the day you'll get dressed.

Poetry Stained Lips

we were once ruled by our tragedies and atrocities until we screamed no more — we began to slowly sew up our bleeding wounds we gathered our inner strength before we could go on — we were drawn to others by the universe, binding us as a tribe — to become warriors day by day until the earth trembled knowing we were no longer a force to be reckoned with

we are now fierce warriors, covering our bodies in war paint, calling to others to fight every battle as one — we not only save ourselves, but we are beginning a legacy to those with no voice, no tribe — alone in this world

but we will give them a home in our tribe of warriors — to show them the way to fight to never be alone again — to pass along our warrior code to every generation after us — we will never surrender no matter the battles, the bruises, the pain that will come from time to time

we are warriors, we are one, one heart, one soul, one voice bound by scars and blood — you will hear us roar

i never believed my heart would betray me — how do i battle love and sensibility

my life is like a simple mixed tape with two sides — side a has my greatest hits, a glimpse of me — but side b is where you will truly find me

Poetry Stained Lips

have you felt your heart break for someone else — to know they are in pain and all you can do is sit with them to try to give comfort but knowing it does not help

to where your heart aches — where you would rip out your own heart and give it to them — to take theirs in return just where they can find peace

for them not to have to endure another moment of crimson tears — staining their cheeks as their lips quiver gasping between breaths

to take a heart broken beyond healing because the wounds of their heart will forever bleed never able to heal or scar

i know for me i would carry your pain until my last breath — if i knew it would make you whole again maybe our lives are not real – maybe it is our souls which have lost their way – only able to exist in these moments – trying over and over to make lifetimes of their wrongs to rights as they try to mold themselves with bits of stardust as galaxies run through their veins, placing themselves in mortal shells – learning about pain, love, and loss – but as they fall, they keep trying while they travel among the stars until the souls can create perfection and give us our very first breath of life – leaving us with their memories – their heavy burdens they endured for lifetimes – where now they can be at peace giving us strength and hope – to be their warriors, their guardians until our last breath

no one really knows my loneliness — i hide it well behind a mask of smiles — reciting the infamous line of i am fine

i carry my loneliness like the worn tattered baby blanket which once warmed me — now it has become a shroud stained with tears and embedded with sobs of yesterday

no matter how much i scrub my skin until it is stinging and raw — i still cannot wash it off — i cannot rinse the bitterness of loneliness from my mouth — it sits upon my tongue, gagging me with its thickness

if only you would look deep in my eyes — into my soul maybe one day i will be found — i doubt the day will ever come

all i can do is breathe in loneliness — my life preserver in a sea that is slowly drowning me i admit i have been wrong — i have been cold i have broken hearts — i have made others cry - i have disappointed — i have spewed venom - i have been selfish — i have been full of rage — i have walked away — i have been ugly — i have been toxic — i could have easily blamed it all on my traumas — my tragedies and continued to be all those things — but a day came where i took a long, hard look in the mirror — i did not like what i saw — i was disgusted — i finally tasted the cold, hard truth of what i was — what i became — i knew i had to face the consequences of my actions — i started to right my wrongs — i knew it was not going to be easy — but they say the first step is always the hardest — i took full responsibility — i have asked for forgiveness even when i knew i did not deserve anyone's kindness — i had to do it — i needed to do it in order to make a change for the better — taking a vow to never be that person again — though i am not perfect — i am fully aware and try like hell to be careful with my words, my actions and if i have hurt anyone now — i am truly sorry and hope you can forgive me

LOVER'S TRIANGLE

Wife

As I sit here alone in the dark with tears that flow
Knowing that he is warming your bed right now
Does he tell you that he loves you - he needs to have you
The promises he made to me - to be mine for all of time
Does he now promise you all those things
Where did it all go wrong for him to seek love in your arms
Will this be the last time he goes to you or is this the end

Mistress

I did not seek him out, he was the one that found me
All I know darlin' is that you destroyed it with him long ago
He comes to my bed whispering how he wants to be inside
Forgetting about all his vows he made to you
I make him feel like a man satisfying all his desires
He promises me that he will leave you soon to be with me
Until then I will send him back to you to live his mundane life

Husband

If you both only knew that I cannot be true to either of you
I have no problem with breaking my vows
Or whispering in your ear what you want to hear
I am getting the best of both worlds
I do not need to give anything in return
Silence from you both is permission for me to keep this up

Poetry Stained Lips

all the colors my soul has been the darkest of hues gives me the most comfort

there are times when i need to use the word fuck in my writings — those four letters — that one-syllable word has expressed more raw emotion than a thousand descriptive words

over time my heart has been shattered – i have always made sure to pick up every broken piece even though it made my fingers bleed – i put each piece away in a worn tattered box – over the years it has collected dust – hoping for the day i can open it back up

hesitant at first to take a chance of mending all those pieces which once caused pain – but i have dusted off that old box and opened it with the hope of second chances for my heart to beat for love instead of pain

every shattered piece now fits perfectly like jigsaw puzzle pieces – creating a beautiful masterpiece of no sadness – only love because each piece interlocked healed a heart by the love i have been given

ABOUT THE AUTHOR

April Spellmeyer began to write when she lost her husband in 2011. When April penned her first piece of poetry the floodgates opened up about loss, grief, mental illness, and trauma. While April expresses in raw, unfiltered emotional imagery she balances it with the beauty of hope, love, strength, and healing.

April uses her writing as a way to bring her words to life and tattoo them on the world.

April is the mother to four children, three fur babies, and Gigi to three grandsons. She enjoys reading, history, Star Wars, and spending time with her family.

April is also the author of Sacrifice & Bloom, and Scars of a Warrior, both available in paperback through the Amazon worldwide marketplace.

You can follow along with her journey on Facebook at facebook.com/aprilyspellmeyer

If you enjoyed this book please consider leaving a review

www.ingramcontent.com/pod-product-compliance
Lightning Source LLC
Chambersburg PA
CBHW070422010526
44118CB00014B/1869